IT'S JUST ME LORD, NOBODY SPECIAL

IT'S JUST ME LORD, NOBODY SPECIAL

Not a fairy tale. Not a sermon. Just one true story about

what God can do with a nobody.

By Tim Rimmer

IT'S JUST ME LORD, NOBODY SPECIAL

GHW
MINISTRIES
www.godshandywork.org

ISBN: 979-8-9988502-0-2
Published by God's Handywork, Inc.
Murfreesboro, Tennessee
Printed in the United States of America

Library of Congress Control Number: 2025909999

DEDICATION

First and foremost, to my Lord and Savior, Jesus Christ, who lovingly guides me along paths I never imagined, transforming every trial into purpose, and shaping me into a vessel He can freely pour from.

To my wife, Yvonne, my best friend, greatest encourager, and constant inspiration—your unwavering love and belief in me have always pushed me to become the man you've seen in me, even when I couldn't see him myself.

And finally, to my late Grandma Taylor, whose gentle wisdom planted seeds of faith long before they blossomed, and who always knew, deep in her heart, that God had a special plan for my life.

foreword

L ife has a way of shaping us—sometimes through hardship, sometimes through grace. For those who have walked through the torment of pain and rejection, it can feel like *your* story is one of struggle alone. But in the hands of God, no past is wasted, no pain goes unseen, and no life is ever *nobody special*.

In his book *It's Just Me Lord, Nobody Special*, Timmy shares his deeply personal journey from a childhood marred by loss and mental and emotional abuse to a life redeemed by faith. As the middle stepchild, he bore the weight of feeling unwanted—labeled a "loser" in a world that often overlooks the quiet battles of a country boy fighting to find his place. And yet, through the trials and hardships, his story is not one of defeat, but of transformation.

I have had the privilege of watching this transformation firsthand. As his wife, I have seen the depth of his struggle—the moments of doubt and the silent battles he fought within himself. I have witnessed, still today, rejection and pain caused by family members and friends who label him a "loser," still not accepting his call. But I have also had a front-row seat to something greater—the undeniable hand of God shaping him into a man of strength, faith, and purpose. The boy who once felt worthless has become a man filled with the love and power of God, walking boldly in his calling as an amazing children's evangelist. His heart, once burdened by rejection, now overflows with compassion for the young souls he reaches. His perseverance and fortitude to share his struggle inspire me, as I know the depth of pain he has faced—pain that some will never see.

But through God's grace, Tim Rimmer not only overcame his past—he stepped into his divine calling, proving that the most broken beginnings can lead to an extraordinary purpose. He has dedicated his life to sharing the Gospel with the young and the young at heart. With a message of love, redemption, and hope, he became an instrument of God's power, proving that even a doubtful heart *can* be used to bring light to others. His story is not merely one of survival, but of transformation and victory. God doesn't just heal our broken pieces—He repurposes them for something great.

This book is not merely a recollection of hardships or short stories—it's a declaration of triumph. It is for anyone who has ever questioned their worth, struggled to rise above the echoes of a painful childhood, or doubted that their life could be used for something greater. It's a prime example of what God can do with a past that seems broken beyond repair. Your pain does not define you. Your past does not limit you. And as Tim Rimmer beautifully illustrates, God has an exceptional way of turning *nobody special* into someone He calls chosen, beloved, and redeemed.

May this story serve as a beacon of hope, reminding us that we are seen, we are loved, and we are part of a godly purpose far greater than we can imagine.

Yvonne Rimmer
A truly blessed and thankful wife

prologue

He wasn't trying to write a book.
He was just trying to make it through.

One school year.

One summer.

One more day of being the stepchild, the overlooked one, the kid with the big feelings and the small voice.

Just Timmy. No titles. No trophies. No spotlight.

He didn't shine.

He survived.

And yet, somehow—somewhere between the skinned knees, the red pants, the kickball line, and the echo of unanswered questions—God saw him.

Not the polished version.

Not the grown-up who learned to laugh it off.

But the boy who often felt invisible.

The one who learned to disappear before anyone ever noticed he was there.

The one who thought maybe he'd been overlooked... even by

God.

That boy.

And this story?

This is his.

A story not about fame, but about faith.
Not about having it all together, but about a God who holds
things together—even when they feel broken beyond repair.

It's not a fairy tale.
It's not a sermon.
It's a scrapbook of truth—messy, beautiful, tender, funny, and
holy in ways only hindsight can reveal.

You'll meet bullies and brothers.
You'll smell honeysuckle and smoke.
You'll laugh, and you'll ache, and you might find yourself
remembering your own barefoot moments.

Because that's the thing about Timmy's story.
It's not just his.

It's the story of anyone who ever felt unseen.
Anyone who ever whispered, "It's just me, Lord. Nobody
special."

If you're looking for a book about a boy with a perfect life,
this isn't it.

Timmy was all boy—and all human.

He messed up.

He got things wrong.

And before he ever stepped into his calling, he was just a sinner in need of saving.

But grace met him anyway.

So here it is.

The rest of the story.

Table of Contents

1 It's a Hard Knock Life.. 1

2 Daddy's Bedtime Stories 7

3 The Wonder Years 13

4 Whose Birthday Is It Anyway? 19

5 Tiger Timmy 25

6 A Brief Embarrassment (That Lasted Forever)............... 31

7 Bapticostal 39

8 Hunky Dory 47

9 Standing in the Need of Prayer 53

10 Let My People Go.. 61

11 Brush Fire.. 71

12 Daddy's Daddy 81

13 Holy Rollers 87

14 Aunt Opal.. 95

15 Where the Wild Things Are................................. 103

16 Where We're Going, We Don't Need Seatbelts 109

17 Aunt Mary Bell 115

18 Thin Line, Big Trouble....................................... 121

19 Wonderful, Magical, No Fuss, Very Best Christmas ... 129

20 Trial by Fire.. 137

21 New School, Same Old Target.............................. 153

22 Country Reflections 161

23 That Ain't No Stick Horse................................... 169

24 Coke and Peanuts 177

25 Frog Giggin' in Etta Bottoms 185

26 One Bike, Two Bike, Timmy's Bike... Gone. 191

27 How the Wind Stole Christmas 201

28 Great Big Tornado... Itty Bitty Living Space.............. 209

29 This Is Gonna Be a Thriller! 219

30 Past Tornado, Stupid Decision 227

31 Well, That Backfired!.. 237

32 Growing Up Under the Stars 247

33 Farther Along 255

34 The Monkey Made Me Do It 263

35 The Ballplayer... 269

36 Crawdad Battles.. 277

37 The Q-Burger Mission 283

38 The Things We Do for a Dollar 293

39 Dare to Be Stupid 301

40 Fade to Black.. 309

41 Sticks and Stones... 323

42 Grandpa Taylor 333

43 Grandma Taylor's Bible 341

44 Where in the World is Tim Rimmer?............................ 347

45 Final Reflection 353

1 IT'S A HARD KNOCK LIFE

The road to Timmy's house didn't look like much. Just a simple stretch of tar and pea gravel, lined with ditches where wildflowers grew between bits of old trash tossed from passing cars. It was rough and sunbaked, the kind of road that could tear up your knees if you tripped—but felt just like home beneath your feet.

In the summer, it shimmered under the hot Arkansas sun, and in the winter, it crunched under the weight of tires—the gravel shifting and settling with every passing car. But to a little boy, that road became something more.

It's Just Me Lord, Nobody Special

It was a racetrack.

A battleground.

A place where adventures were born.

His first home, the one he first remembered, sat just off that
road—a modest little white house with paneled walls and square
white ceiling tiles that muffled every creak and whisper.

Out front, the porch collected everything from stray kittens
to rusting bicycles.

The yard was surrounded by beautiful mimosa trees, their
pink blossoms filling the air with a sweet aroma every spring.
But not everything in that yard was so welcoming—hidden
beneath the grass was a patch of stickers, and Timmy learned the
hard way to avoid running through it barefoot. One wrong step,
and you'd suffer for it.

Barbara, his stepmother, was a stay-at-home wife who took
in children to babysit on the side.
Elton, his daddy, was short and stocky, with thinning brown hair
and a thick, bristly beard that made him look a little like a grizzly
bear. But under all that scruff and grease, he had the quiet heart
of a teddy bear. He came home every evening smelling of dirt
and oil, his hands rough and stained from a long day at the

wrecking yard—but his presence always brought a kind of calm, even if he didn't say much. Jerry, the oldest, was smart and quiet—usually tucked away in his room with a stack of comic books, unless he was picking fights with his younger brothers. Jessie, the youngest, was Barbara's son. He had a mischievous streak and a laugh that could be heard clear across the yard— loud, restless, always in motion, always getting Timmy into trouble.

And Timmy—well, he was just trying to find his place in the mix. He had a lot of questions about the world—big ones—but nobody ever seemed to have the time or the patience to answer them. Why did grown-ups always tell kids to tell the truth, but then get mad when they didn't like the answer?

Why did some people live in big houses while others barely had enough to get by?

Why did some kids have mamas who tucked them in at night, while others only saw theirs on certain weekends?

Why did it feel like he was always one step behind—like he wasn't as fast, as funny, or as smart as the other kids?

Maybe being left out was just the way things worked. Some people were special. Some people weren't.

And maybe Timmy just wasn't.

But for all the things he didn't understand, one thing was certain—Timmy had an imagination.

He could turn a rusted-out sedan in the yard into a spaceship, complete with buttons and launch codes. A ditch became the Grand Canyon, wide and daring. The old wringer washing machine near the old chicken coop? That was his ice cream stand.

With a flick of the wrist and a creaky turn of the crank, Timmy would serve pretend cones to pretend customers with very real enthusiasm. "One chocolate swirl," he'd say, handing air to a group of friends he wished he had. "Extra sprinkles? Sure thing."

Sometimes he'd even shout out the daily special—"Two scoops for the price of one!"

And when business slowed, he headed out back to ride bulls—or rather, one giant, sun-bleached butane tank. He'd straddle it like a cowboy in a rodeo, one hand in the air, the other gripping tight.

"Eight seconds!" he'd shout to the wind.

"New record!"

The tank didn't buck. It didn't move at all. But in Timmy's world, it was the meanest bull this side of the Mississippi.

The world outside might've been small. But the one inside his mind? That one was big enough for heroes and monsters, spaceships, and moon landings.

And while the world was racing to the moon, Timmy was just trying to survive the monsters under his bed.

But there was a problem.

Timmy was a nobody.

At least, that was the assumption he built from the feedback around him.

At school he was the laughingstock of the playground, yes—but the bullying didn't stop there. It was at home, too—from a stepmom who said he would never amount to anything.

And so, as he got down on his knees at night to say his bedtime prayers, he would start with the only words that ever seemed to fit:

Hello, Lord… it's just me. Nobody special.

He hadn't been told yet—not by the right person, anyway—that God had a plan for him.

But his Grandma Taylor, she already knew.

At night, though… at night, things were different. Because when the sun went down and the house settled into the quiet hum of bedtime, Daddy told stories.

And suddenly, Timmy wasn't just a boy in a small town anymore.

He was wherever the stories took him.

And as Daddy's voice carried into the night, something inside Timmy stirred.

Something he wouldn't fully understand until many years later.

Because stories—the right stories—have a way of changing everything.

Even for a nobody.

2 DADDY'S BEDTIME STORIES

Nighttime at the house on the tar-and-pea-gravel road was like a soft reset on the day. The noise of childhood faded into the hum of box fans in the windows, the smell of supper still lingering in the air. Dishes stacked neatly in the drainer, a tea glass sweating on the table. The babysitting kids had all gone home. Jerry and Jessie had settled into their beds. The television in the living room flickered softly in the background, but in the bedroom, everything was still.

The window was cracked just enough to let in the scent of honeysuckle from the fence line, mixed with the distant smell of rain on dirt. Somewhere far off, a dog barked once, then again.

The stillness wasn't silent—it breathed. It waited. It held space for something sacred.

Timmy, perched on the top bunk, waited for his favorite part of the day.

Because every night, without fail, Daddy told stories.

They weren't read from a book. Daddy didn't need a book. He carried every tale in his memory, like a vault of adventures just waiting to be unlocked. He made them come alive, painting pictures with words, making the characters as real as the walls around them.

The stories were never rushed. Each one unfolded like a miniature stage play. Daddy changed his voice for every character, drawing out suspense, making them laugh, making them listen. His voice could dip low and gravelly or rise into a squeaky pitch with a snap of transformation, as if the people in the stories had stepped right into the room.

Even the shadows seemed to lean in, like the room itself was holding its breath between Daddy's words. Timmy noticed how the hall light cast a glow that stopped just short of the bunk bed—like the rest of the house knew to leave this part untouched.

Timmy and Jessie shared a bedroom, and though they had bunk beds, only one bed really mattered at story time—the bottom bunk. Timmy would drape himself over the edge, his head hanging down, watching the world upside down while Jessie lay stretched out below. Sometimes Jessie would reach up and flick Timmy's hair, and Timmy would swat his hand and yell at him to stop, all while grinning the whole time.

Their giggles were quiet but contagious. Sometimes it took Daddy a moment to get them to settle down before starting. He never scolded, though. He just waited with a patient smirk, arms crossed, like a performer letting the crowd quiet itself.

And there, in that small room with paneling on the walls and water-stained white square tiles on the ceiling, a father wove magic from nothing but words.

The classics made their rounds—*Goldilocks and the Three Bears, The Three Little Pigs*—but Daddy had his own favorites. One of them was about a fat man.

"Fat man, fat man, what makes you so fat?" Daddy would persist, his voice teasing, setting the stage.

And every time, no matter how often he told it, Timmy laughed before he even got to the punchline. He couldn't help it. It wasn't just the story—it was Daddy's voice, the silly faces he made, the way his eyes lit up when he delivered the line. Sometimes Daddy would toss in a new word or twist, just enough to make it feel like a surprise. And even when it wasn't, it still was. That was part of the charm—knowing what was coming and loving it anyway.

Some nights, it was *The Three Billy Goats Gruff*. And oh, how Daddy loved to play the part of the troll under the bridge. "Who's that walking over my bridge?" he would bellow, deep and gruff.

Jessie would gasp. Timmy would grab onto the bunk railing, eyes wide, knowing what came next.

"It is I! The littlest billy goat!" Daddy would squeak, his voice high-pitched and nervous.

The story never changed, but somehow, Daddy's version never got old. Maybe it was because the voices made the room come alive, or maybe it was because Daddy loved telling them just as much as the boys loved hearing them.

Or maybe—just maybe—it was because, in those moments, everything felt right. The stories didn't fix anything. They didn't change what tomorrow might hold. But they built a world where

Timmy was safe, where he could laugh, where he could believe in trolls and goats and fat men with funny names.

And on the best nights—the ones Timmy would never forget—Daddy made up his own stories. Ones no one else had ever heard before. Stories about places they'd never seen and people with names that made them laugh until their sides hurt. Aliens that ran gas stations. A cat who played the harmonica. A runaway pancake that tricked a whole town. The plot didn't matter. The joy was in the telling.

In those moments, nothing else mattered—not the hard days,

not the bullies at school,

not the feeling of being small in a world that didn't seem to notice him.

Because in those moments, Daddy's stories made him feel like he belonged to something bigger.

Timmy didn't realize it at the time, but those stories—the ones told in the dark, in the safety of that tiny room—were shaping him. They were becoming part of him.

They soaked in, slow and invisible, the way warmth seeps into your bones when you sit too close to the fire. Years later, when everything else blurred, these stories would remain sharp and clear, like stars on a cold night.

And before the last echoes of the troll's angry roar disappeared into the night, Timmy and Jessie would drift off, carried away by the magic of Daddy's bedtime stories.

They didn't know it then.

Didn't realize how precious those moments were.

How quickly time would pass.

How one day, the stories would stop.

That voice—the voice of Daddy telling stories in the dark— would never leave them.

And that, more than anything, was the greatest story of all.

Sometimes, years later, Timmy would catch himself smiling for no reason and realize it was because of those nights. Even if the world outside was unpredictable—even if school was hard and Barbara's moods were harder, even if money was tight and the house was cold—inside those stories, anything was possible.

The stories Daddy told were full of wonder—just like those early years of Timmy's life.

Or at least… the parts he could still remember.

3 THE WONDER YEARS

Timmy remembered first grade. Not every detail—not every day—but enough to know it happened. And not just happened—it mattered.

He could still picture the back row of Mrs. Laney's classroom at Magnet Cove Elementary, where he sat in a stiff wooden chair, legs dangling, sneakers barely brushing the floor. The scent of pencil shavings, chalk dust, and construction paper hung in the air, mingling with the distant echoes of laughter and kickball—sounds drifting in from the upper grades out on the playground.

His favorite part of the day was the books.

That year, Timmy learned how to read—not just to sound out words, but to truly understand them.

His favorite was *Tip and Mitten*—a story about a dog and a cat, filled with simple sentences and soft drawings that made the world feel safe. *"See Tip, See Tip run, run Tip run"* Timmy would flip each page like he was opening a treasure chest—each word a shiny coin he never knew he had.

There were others too: *Jack and Janet, Dick and Jane.*
They weren't exactly thrilling.
But they were warm.
Predictable.
Comforting.

First grade was also where Timmy learned to write his name. He practiced carefully on his Big Chief writing pad, the thick red kind with wide lines and feathered paper. His extra-large pencil felt like a log in his small hands, but he gripped it tight and made each letter count. He kept his pencils in a King Edward cigar box that he brought with him to school—just like some of the other boys did. It wasn't fancy, but it held his treasures: pencils, crayons, and sometimes even a few of the cute rocks he picked up on the playground.

Before anything else, every morning began the same way:

Hands over hearts, voices united in the Pledge of Allegiance.

And then, without hesitation—a prayer.

Right there in public school. No one argued. No one called a

meeting. It was just what you did.

And for Timmy, it planted the seed of something good—

something grounding—before life had a chance to uproot it.

That was first grade. The part that stayed.

But second grade?

Third grade?

Gone.

Like someone had yanked the film from the reel and left behind

a blank screen.

He searched and searched, year after year, trying to find a

thread—just one image to bring those years into focus.

But there was nothing.

No teacher names. No classmates. No moments.

He flipped through old yearbooks once, squinting at the

grainy, black-and-white photos.

"There I am." he thought

"There's my name—Timmy Rimmer. That's me.

I knew I was alive… but I don't remember living it."

Were those years just dull?

Were they normal, nothing-special, in-between kinds of years?

Or were they so hard—so lonely, so confusing—that his mind

did the only thing it could to survive?

Maybe both.

Maybe some years are quiet on the outside and chaotic on

the inside.

And maybe that chaos doesn't leave marks you can see—just

blank spaces where memories should be.

The only thing he remembered—the one and only clue—

was cursive.

Timmy could still see the blue-lined paper with extra-wide

spacing.

He remembered holding his pencil tight, tongue poking out the

side of his mouth as he tried to loop the letters just right.

Capital Qs that looked like the number 2 in a cartoon.

Lowercase z's that didn't look like anything at all.

Page after page of swirls and squiggles, all in the name of

penmanship.

That was it.

That was the only surviving fragment from two entire years of school.

Cursive.

Sometimes he'd laugh about it—how of all the things to remember, that's what stuck.

And sometimes he wouldn't laugh at all.

Because the truth was, he wanted to remember.

Even the bad parts.

Even the awkward, embarrassing, painful ones.

But you can't make memories happen.

You can only notice the ones that show up.

And the ones that didn't?

Well, those were ghosts.

Not scary. Not loud.

Just absent.

Maybe that's why first grade glowed so brightly in his mind. Not because it was perfect—he was still the kid in hand-me-downs, still shy, still unsure—but because it was there.

It was real.

And maybe that's the strange truth about "the wonder years."

They're not always full of wonder.

Sometimes, they're full of wondering.

Where was I?

Why can't I remember?

And what does that missing silence say about the boy I was becoming?

Maybe the silence was trying to protect him.

Or maybe it was just making room for the memories that came next.

The ones that didn't disappear.

The ones that stuck—like a birthday that wasn't really his.

4 WHOSE BIRTHDAY IS IT ANYWAY?

It was May 5th, 1976—Timmy's eighth birthday. In just a few months, he'd be starting third grade.

He'd been waiting all day, playing in the yard close to the road, staring up the hill every time he heard a vehicle approaching. Each sound sent his heart racing. This was the day. Daddy would be pulling into the driveway soon—and with any luck, there'd be a gift involved. Not just any gift. A good one. Maybe even something brand new... not a hand-me-down.

The road in front of their house was paved the country way—first a layer of black tar, then a topcoat of pea gravel. Over time, traffic had packed it down into a smooth, hard surface. Timmy watched it shimmer in the Arkansas heat, waiting for the first sign of his Daddy's truck popping up over the top of the hill.

Finally, he could hear it—the low hum of the old pickup truck rolling up the gravel. Timmy raced up the driveway next to the beat-up Ford, waiting for him to park and swing open the door. Elton sat on the edge of the seat, arm resting on the open window, grinning like he had a secret.

Daddy looked at him and said, "Pick a color."

Timmy blinked. "Uh… red?"

Daddy shook his head. "Nope. Try again."

"Green?"

"Nope."

Timmy tilted his head. "Yellow?"

Daddy's grin stretched wider. He leaned over and pulled a yellow skateboard from behind the seat. Timmy's eyes lit up.

It wasn't the fanciest board—a flat plank with a rounded front, thick plastic wheels, and a slick deck. But it was his. Yellow, with bright red wheels. Brand new.

Before he could fully take it in, Jessie—riding his Big Wheel around the yard—leapt up and came running over to see

Timmy's new board.

"Pick a color," Daddy said to him.

Timmy's stomach dropped.

"Blue!" Jessie said, and out came a blue skateboard, just like Timmy's.

Then Jerry, having made his way out of his bedroom where his face had been buried in a stack of comic books, called out, "How about black?"

Daddy laughed again and pulled a black skateboard out from behind the seat.

Timmy stood there, holding his yellow board, watching his brothers laugh and spin the tires on theirs. The birthday glow dimmed.

He didn't say anything. He didn't cry. But it stung.

"Why does everyone get a present on my birthday?" he wondered.

But that was the way it always went for Timmy—being the middle child meant sharing the spotlight, even on the one day that was supposed to be his.

It's Just Me Lord, Nobody Special

They didn't even ask what his favorite color was. He would've picked blue. But he didn't know it was a guessing game.

He followed his brothers down the driveway, each of them carrying their boards. Up the road, the hill waited. Not too steep, but steep enough to make your stomach flutter if you caught the speed just right. The bottom ended at a one-lane wooden bridge—rickety, weathered, and just narrow enough to make you nervous.

The boys climbed to the top. Jerry went first—standing upright, knees bent just like the skateboarders on TV. He whooshed down the hill like he'd done it a hundred times.

Jessie followed close behind, a little more reluctant, but still arms out wide, yelling something about being faster than Evel Knievel.

Timmy stood at the top, clutching his yellow board.
He looked down.
That bridge was coming up fast at the bottom of the hill. If you didn't stop in time, you risked flying off or slamming into the wooden railings. The thought alone made his chest tighten.

He swallowed hard.

There was no way he could stand up and ride it like the others. Not today. Maybe not ever.

So, he laid his board down flat, dropped onto his stomach, and stretched his arms out like airplane wings. His face was just inches from the pavement.

He gave a push and took off.

The red wheels buzzed against the smooth gravel—a high-pitched hum rising like a swarm of bees, growing louder as the hill pulled him faster and faster. The wind whipped past his ears, tugging at his shirt, stinging his eyes. Every bump in the road rattled through his elbows. Pebbles pinged off the board like tiny missiles. His nose filled with the hot, tarry scent of summer and dust. He gritted his teeth and held on.

And then—the bridge loomed ahead. Timmy dug his heels into the gravel, trying to slow down. The board wobbled. His stomach dropped. At the very last second, just before hitting the lip of the bridge, the board skidded to a stop. He rolled off into the grass, heart pounding. Close call.

But he'd done it.

He lay there for a moment, catching his breath, staring up at the blue sky, still trembling from the rush. It wasn't graceful, and it sure wasn't cool—but it was his ride. His way.

That's how it always went—not flashy, not first—but fearless in his own quiet way.

Back up the hill, his brothers were already lining up for another run. Daddy leaned against the truck, watching. Timmy dusted off his shirt and carried his board back up the hill. He didn't need applause. He didn't need praise.

What he needed—what he got—was a moment of courage. And maybe, just maybe, that was the real gift that day. Not the yellow skateboard. Not the red wheels. But the quiet, stubborn decision to ride anyway—even if nobody noticed. Even if it wasn't fair.

Because Timmy had learned something. In a house full of brothers, birthdays weren't really about the presents. They were about how you handled the ride.

He didn't get the biggest gift. He didn't even get his favorite color. But he got something else. Something quiet. Something that settled deep inside him and stayed.

Spend enough time on the edges though, and the spotlight doesn't feel like a reward—it feels like a trap…

5 TIGER TIMMY

It was just another typical school day at Magnet Cove Elementary.

The sun beamed down through the classroom windows, casting warm patches of light on the desks. Outside, the leaves on the big oak trees rustled in a lazy breeze, hinting that recess was just around the corner. Somewhere in the distance, the faint hum of a lawnmower drifted through the open windows, mixing with the scratch of pencils on paper and the occasional shuffle of restless feet.

Timmy's mind wasn't on the lesson.

His main thought? What was on the lunch menu.

It's Just Me Lord, Nobody Special

If it was Salisbury steak day, he'd have to make peace with a meal of mashed potatoes and a buttered roll. But if it was pizza day? Oh, now that was something to look forward to.

And then—there was recess.

It was sno-cone day.

All you needed was ten cents to get an icy, syrupy treat, and Timmy had been saving his dime all week. He could already taste the sugary goodness melting on his tongue, the way it turned his lips bright red or electric blue, depending on the flavor.

His favorite was Rainbow.

But before the bell rang—before recess and sno-cones and whatever mystery meal awaited in the cafeteria—there was Gregg Mason.

Gregg wasn't particularly big. In fact, he was scrawny. But what he lacked in size, he made up for in relentlessness.

Every day, without fail, Gregg found a way to make Timmy's life miserable—tripping him in the hallway, knocking books from his hands, taunting him in front of the other kids.

Timmy had been taught to turn the other cheek.

To walk away.

To be the bigger person.

And so, he did.

Until the day he didn't.

Timmy only had two cheeks—and both had already been turned.

It started in the classroom, just before the bell rang for recess. Gregg was already pushing his limits, running his mouth, testing how far he could go.

Then the bell rang. And the second they stepped outside, Gregg came right at him.

Timmy knew—this time he had to fight back.

Without thinking, without planning—he swung.

One punch.

One moment of defiance.

His fist connected—not hard, not clean, but enough to shock them both. His hand stung, and his ears rang from the sudden shout of the kids around them.

And just like that—Gregg backed down.

Timmy froze.

Was he in trouble?

He turned toward Mrs. Overton, waiting for the scolding, the punishment.

But she said nothing.

Not yet.

The kids around him were still whispering, still watching. But Timmy wasn't thinking about them.

His heart was hammering in his chest.

Gregg had slunk away, but was that really the end of it? Would he come back swinging?

Would a teacher suddenly appear and drag Timmy inside by the arm?

He didn't want to be around the other kids. Not now. So, he climbed the tall slide at the far end of the playground, perched himself at the top, and sat there—legs pulled in, arms wrapped around his knees.

From up there, he could see the whole playground—every pocket of kids playing, every kickball rolling across the dirt. It felt safer being above it all. Like he could breathe again. Like maybe, just maybe, he wasn't the smallest kid on the playground today.

And more importantly, he could see Gregg.

He kept his eyes on him, watching for any sign that the fight wasn't really over.

Minutes dragged by.

No one came for him.

Gregg didn't look his way.

Finally, the bell rang, and recess was over.

Timmy slid down; his legs were still shaky.

The students rushed back inside, the air still buzzing from what they had just witnessed.

Timmy sat down at his desk, his tiny hands still curled into fists beneath the table.

Then Mrs. Overton walked past his desk.

She didn't scold him. Didn't send him to the principal's office.

She simply looked him straight in the eye and said, "Well, look at you, Tiger Timmy."

She didn't smile, exactly. But there was no anger in her voice—only something like quiet approval.

Timmy was stunned.

Tiger Timmy?

Was this for real?

She must have seen Gregg giving him trouble before.

Maybe she was glad to see him finally stand up for himself.

And for that one day—just one day—Timmy wasn't the victim.

He was Tiger Timmy.

He had finally found his roar on the playground.

Of course, it didn't last.

The next day, things went back to normal.

The bullying only stopped for a little while.

And though Gregg left him alone—for now—Timmy never stopped looking over his shoulder.

Because playground victories?

They're temporary.

And sometimes, the next blow doesn't come with fists...

6 A Brief Embarrassment (That Lasted Forever)

Some memories fade, dissolving into the background noise of time. Others cling to you like a stubborn burr—tiny, sharp, impossible to forget. For Timmy, there was one day in fourth grade that never really let go. It wasn't loud or dramatic, not at first. But it had teeth. And it bit deep.

It started the way most school days did—grabbing whatever clean-ish clothes were closest, getting dressed without much thought. His Fruit of the Loom underwear, still slightly stiff from line drying, didn't raise any red flags. Why would they? Underwear was supposed to stay private. Hidden. Safe from the spotlight.

What Timmy didn't know was that somewhere in the laundry pile, a brand-new pair of blue jeans had bled during the wash. His tighty-whities—just another item accidentally tossed in with the colors—came out tinted blue.

It was just a mistake. His stepmom hadn't meant to do it. And Timmy, not thinking twice, wore them to school.

Because who's going to see your underwear?

Until they do.

The sun was already high by the time P.E. rolled around, baking the Arkansas clay into a dusty red crust. The students trudged outside, grumbling under their breath, wiping sweat off their foreheads before the first whistle even blew. Timmy stayed near the back of the line. P.E. wasn't his scene. He wasn't fast. He wasn't coordinated. And he definitely wasn't one of the cool kids. His main goal during gym class was to survive it as invisibly as possible.

Today, though, there was a surprise. Coach had rolled out the big parachute—a faded rainbow-colored monstrosity that only came out a few times a year. Instantly, the energy shifted. Kids squealed and ran toward it like moths to a porch light, already shouting about popcorn and mushroom domes and who would go under first.

For once, Timmy felt like he could just be part of something. No teams. No picking sides. Just everyone holding a slice of fabric and bouncing a ball together.

He took his place at the edge, gripping the hem tight between his fingers. The game began—lift, snap, ripple, bounce. Laughter filled the air. The fabric snapped in the breeze.

Even Timmy smiled, watching the ball dance in the middle like it was alive.

Then came the moment everyone waited for—the signal to lift the parachute high and dive underneath, trapping the air and creating a billowing dome of color overhead.

Inside, it was quiet. Hushed. Magical.

Timmy knelt on the grass, watching the sunlight filter through the nylon above, casting patches of red and blue and yellow over the laughing faces around him. The air smelled faintly of cut grass and sneakers. His hands were damp. His knees itched. But he didn't care.

He belonged. For once.

That's when it happened.

A hand grabbed the waistband of his shorts—and yanked it skyward.

A wedgie.

It happened so fast he didn't even have time to react—but what came next felt like it unfolded in slow motion.

"Timmy's got blue underwear!" someone hollered, already laughing before the words even finished leaving their mouth.

The words rang out—loud and clear.

Timmy's heart sank.

Someone—maybe Gregg Mason—had just announced to everyone what no one was ever supposed to see.

And by the time they crawled back out into the sunlight, the chant had already begun.

"Timmy's got blue underwear! Timmy's got blue underwear!"

Over and over.

The chant grew louder. Fingers pointed. Laughter spread like wildfire.

Timmy stood frozen. Face flushed. Hands clenched.

He couldn't speak. Couldn't move. Every muscle in his body wanted to disappear.

But there was nowhere to go.

The parachute—once a place of fun and hiding—had become a stage. And Timmy was the punchline.

Finally, Ms. Ehrgood reached for the silver whistle hanging around her neck, the one that usually hung silent unless chaos broke out.

She brought it to her lips, took a deep breath, and blew.

The shriek of the whistle cut through the chanting like a knife. It was sharp, sudden, and piercing—louder than laughter, louder than footsteps, louder than shame.

Every head snapped toward her.

The sound didn't ask for attention—it demanded it.

The chanting stumbled. Then stopped.

A few kids looked around, sheepish. Others smirked, still riding the high of the moment.

But none of them said another word.

Ms. Ehrgood didn't have to yell. The whistle did it for her.

But the damage was done.

Because it wasn't just underwear anymore. It was him.

The boy with the blue underwear. The joke. The nobody.

And even now, all these years later… Even though the faces have faded, and the voices are harder to place… That moment never really left.

Because it doesn't always take a punch to leave a bruise.

Sometimes it just takes—one careless wash. One cruel chant. One silent walk back to the building…

to convince a kid that he's not like the others. That he's less than. That he doesn't belong.

But Timmy didn't show it. He didn't cry. He didn't tattle.

He just walked back across the red dirt, feeling the weight of invisible eyes on his back.

Not one of them knew what it felt like—to be seen like that.

Not one of them knew what it would cost.

And what hurt the most… Wasn't the wedgie. Or the chant. Or even the fact that Ms. Ehrgood had to make them stop.

It was how easy it was for them to turn on him. How quickly they laughed. How fast they forgot he was a person.

Timmy didn't find safety in school that day. Not in the classroom. Not on the track. Not under the parachute.

And at home, things weren't much better.

But there was one place—one time of the week—that felt different. Not perfect. Not predictable. Not even peaceful, always.

But different.

A different kind of attention. A different kind of noise.

Because on Sunday mornings, everything changed—depending on which parent had custody that weekend.

7 Bapticostal

If there was one thing set in stone for Timmy while growing up in Arkansas, it was that Sunday was church day. No ifs, ands, or buts about it.

On Sunday mornings, the family followed the same routine like clockwork. They would squeeze into their best clothes, pile into the car, and head down the road to church.

The day began with Sunday school, where Timmy and the other kids sat through Bible lessons that seemed to last forever. But at 11:00 sharp, the bell would ring, and everyone gathered in the church sanctuary.

Timmy would sit beside his daddy, fidgeting with anything he could get his hands on—his shoelaces, the edge of the pew, even the chewing gum stuck underneath. Anything to stay occupied while the preacher babbled on.

But then, the moment he had been waiting for arrived. The song director would step up, hymnbook in hand, and in a voice that sounded like he had been gargling gravel, he'd announce:

"Turn to page such-and-such. We'll sing the first and second verses and stand on the last."

Timmy always found this fascinating.

What was wrong with the third verse? He wondered.

Was it not good enough? Was it hiding something?

He had once peeked ahead in the hymnal, but the words seemed normal enough. Still, rules were rules. First and second only—and everyone stood on the last. That was just how it was done.

But for Timmy, Sundays weren't always the same. Because every other weekend, him and Jerry went to visit their mom, Ella—and she had her own Sunday tradition.

And that's when things got interesting.

Church started the same way as always: Sunday school first, then worship in the main sanctuary.

But as soon as they walked in, Timmy knew something was different.

The moment the pianist's fingers slammed down on the keys; the entire congregation exploded to their feet.

Timmy's eyes widened.

Wait… are we starting with the last verse?

He barely had time to process it before the people around him began clapping—loudly.

Are we even allowed to do this? He wondered.

But before he could finish that thought, he noticed something even stranger.

Across the congregation, people had their hands lifted high, reaching toward the ceiling like they were trying to grab something. Some were jumping up and down. Others were swaying with their eyes closed.

And then, to Timmy's complete and utter amazement, they started dancing!

His jaw nearly hit the floor.

"Daddy is never gonna believe this!" he thought.

And then came the preaching.

The man behind the big wooden pulpit cracked open his Bible

and started reading. At first, he spoke in a normal voice. But as he continued, his tone rose—louder and louder—until he was practically shouting.

Timmy stiffened.

"Why is he yelling?" Timmy wondered.

And then, to his shock, people started yelling back!

Timmy listened carefully. It sounded like they were shouting, "Hey man!"—like they were trying to get his attention or tell him to hush.

Timmy gulped.

"Y'all are about to get in trouble!"

But to his utter confusion, the preacher didn't stop.

He got even louder!

And the people?

They weren't upset at all—they were shouting even more!

And then, just when Timmy thought things couldn't get any stranger...

Someone near the front suddenly burst out with a sound Timmy didn't recognize—a string of syllables that didn't sound like English at all.

His head turned sharply.

"Was that another language?" he wondered.

"Are they from another country?"

The people around them didn't flinch. In fact, some nodded. Others lifted their hands higher.

Timmy sat frozen, trying to figure out what was going on.

Coming here was like stepping into another world.

Timmy's nine-year-old brain was spinning.

This was a lot to comprehend.

At the Baptist church, the biggest excitement was when Brother Boatwright fell asleep and started snoring mid-sermon. But this place—people were feeling something.

Timmy sat there, completely bewildered.

This wasn't like the church Daddy took him to.

Not one bit.

It wasn't the church where you sang a couple of verses, stood on the last, and listened to a preacher who spoke in a calm, even tone.

But the Pentecostals didn't stop at just two verses. They sang every single one—and if the Spirit was moving, they circled back and did it all again.

It's Just Me Lord, Nobody Special

The preacher didn't just talk—he roared from the pulpit, stomping and sweating, swinging his arms like he was trying to swat the devil himself!

And Timmy?

Well, Timmy sat there, taking it all in, trying to make sense of a world where church could be this exciting.

That Sunday, nine-year-old Timmy got his first taste of a different kind of church.

It was the first time.

But it wouldn't be the last.

For years, Timmy straddled both worlds.

One weekend? Baptist.

The next? Pentecostal.

Two churches.

Two experiences.

Two different ways of worship.

And at some point, something became clear.

He wasn't just one or the other.

He was BAPTICOSTAL.

For Timmy, church—whatever kind it was—belonged to Sunday.

But the rest of the week?

The rest of the week was for running barefoot down dirt roads, cooling off in the creek, and getting into just enough mischief to keep things interesting.

And on one particular sweltering summer day, Timmy and his cousins found out just how far one determined dog would go to catch a ride...

8 HUNKY DORY

Summer in Arkansas brought its own kind of battles—not the kind fought with fists or words—but with sweat-soaked shirts and sunburned necks.

The air was thick enough to chew, and the cicadas sang so loud they could drown out your own thoughts.

Shade was currency. Water was salvation.

And on the hottest days, there was only one place to escape it—Big Rock.

The creek wasn't deep, but it was cold—bone-chilling even in the middle of July. The water flowed clear over smooth stones, slippery as soap under bare feet. Minnows darted

between shadows, and dragonflies hovered above like tiny
helicopters on patrol.

It was a creek lined with trees, winding its way through the
woods—and right in the middle, a giant rock.
Not your average rock—this one rose like a tower from the
creek, standing at least five feet tall. If you were lucky, you could
scramble up and perch on that rock, watching the water rush
past as the world slowed down just for a moment.

One summer day, after a morning of hard work, a group of
cousins showed up at Timmy's house, ready for a swim. No time
to waste. They piled into the old pickup truck, just like families
did back then. Some sat on the tailgate, others bounced in the
bed, heading down the gravel road toward their favorite spot—
Big Rock.

But there was a twist in the plan—one that no one saw
coming.
Hunky Dory, the family pet, came tearing around the corner like
a black bullet with ears, tongue lolling sideways, like he'd just
escaped prison.

He wasn't just chasing the truck—he was chasing destiny.

Anyone who had spent a day at their house knew—Hunky Dory wasn't just any dog. He was stubborn, determined, and when he set his sights on something, not even a pickup truck could stop him.

As the truck made its way down the road, Hunky Dory kept running, his paws pounding the hot gravel. Faster and faster, he pushed himself—not willing to be left behind.

But then it happened.

One second, he was a blur of motion. The next, he was flat on the gravel—legs splayed like a cartoon, eyes half-closed, tongue hanging long and dramatic.

A chorus of gasps rose from the truck bed.

"Stop! Stop! Hunky Dory's hurt!" came the cry from the back of the truck. Panic set in. The driver slammed on the brakes, the truck screeching to a halt.

In reverse they went, bouncing back to where the dog lay. For a heartbeat, nobody moved. The truck creaked to a stop. Gravel crunched under panicked footsteps. Someone yelled for water. Another was already crying.

Then—like Lazarus from the grave—Hunky Dory sprang to life.

With a wag of his tail, he bounded into the bed of the truck like nothing had ever happened.

And there, as the truth set in, the children realized that Hunky Dory hadn't been hurt at all.

No—he'd faked an injury just to get them to stop and let him catch a ride to Big Rock.

The rest of the family, once they'd recovered from the shock, continued their journey. When they reached Big Rock, Hunky Dory wasted no time diving into the cool waters, swimming alongside the kids with the joy of a dog who had just pulled off the greatest stunt of the summer.

And from that day on, nobody ever left for Big Rock without checking the rearview mirror—for a black blur running after them with one goal in mind: to ride in style.

And as for Big Rock—well, it would never be the same without the memory of that day, when a dog proved that sometimes, the greatest adventures come from the most unexpected tricks.

The weekend was over, but summer still stretched out ahead of them.

When the cousins packed up and left, the house got too quiet.

The screen door slammed with less purpose.

The yard felt emptier.

And without the cool creek or the chaos of family, Timmy found himself pacing the yard, looking for anything—to chase the boredom away.

The joy of the swim, the prank of the dog, the warmth of family—it all faded too quickly.

And what lingered was the echo of being left behind.

He didn't have the words for it yet. Not fully.

But soon, he would.

In the most unexpected place…

With a song.

And a prayer.

9 STANDING IN THE NEED OF PRAYER

Vacation Bible School was supposed to be fun. And in a way, it was. There were crafts, snacks, games, and loud songs with hand motions. Volunteers wore big smiles and bright shirts, doing their best to wrangle a room full of kids hopped up on oversweetened red Kool-Aid and graham crackers. The fellowship hall buzzed with the sounds of squeaky sneakers, crinkling paper, and off-key singing.

To most kids, it was heaven.

But not for Timmy.

To Timmy, it was just another place to feel small.

It's Just Me Lord, Nobody Special

He wasn't the funny one.

Wasn't the cool one.

Wasn't even the one anybody noticed.

He was just… there.

A shadow in the corner.

A face without a name.

A nobody.

Even in a room full of kids, Timmy felt invisible.

The song leader stood at the front with laminated signs—

"STOP" and "GO"—and the kids shouted and stomped

through the lyrics like it was a race to the finish.

"Stop and let me tell you what the Lord has done for me…"

"Go and tell the story of the Christ of Calvary…"

Timmy sang along, half a beat behind, mouthing the words

because everyone else was.

It was just what you did.

Then came the Band-Aid song—

"I'm in love with Jesus 'cause Jesus first loved me…"

Sung to a jingle from a TV commercial.

There was laughter. Clapping. Giggles.

A parody of the Oscar Mayer commercial followed—

"I wish I was like Jesus Christ, my Savior…"

More laughter. Louder now.

Timmy sat still.

Something inside him was pulling back.

Like he was present—but not part of it.

And then came the song that changed everything.

"It's me, it's me, O Lord, standing in the need of prayer…"

"Not my mother, not my father, but it's me, O Lord…"

Those words hit differently.

They didn't bounce off the walls like the others.

They landed.

It's me, O Lord…

Not anyone else.

Not the noisy kids.

Not the smiling volunteers.

Not even the teachers who called him by the wrong name.

Just Timmy—The boy nobody picked.

The boy who didn't know where he fit.

The boy who didn't get answers—only silence.

The one who got laughed at, at home and at school… and even

here.

It's Just Me Lord, Nobody Special

He couldn't take it anymore.

So, he slipped out. Quietly.

No one noticed.

Not one person stopped him.

That's how invisible he was.

The sun had already gone down. The parking lot was dim, lit only by a buzzing streetlamp and the warm glow spilling out from the fellowship hall windows. Laughter still echoed faintly from inside—bright, happy noise that didn't match how Timmy felt.

He wandered over to a bench just beyond the lights. Far enough away to be alone. Close enough to still hear the song echoing in his mind.

And he sat down.

No games—

No shouting—

No paper crowns or popsicle sticks.

Just Timmy. Alone in the dark.

And he began to sing—softly.

Not for anyone else.

Not because he was told to.

But because the words were true.

"It's me, it's me, O Lord..."

"Standing in the need of prayer..."

And in that moment—God came.

He could have stayed inside, in the fellowship hall,

surrounded by all the other kids—the ninety-nine.

But He didn't.

He came for the one.

The quiet one who slipped out unnoticed.

The lonely one on a bench under the night sky.

The lost one—standing in the need of prayer.

And God saw him.

Not the crowd.

Not the motions.

Not the performance.

Just Timmy.

Small.

Forgotten.

Unimportant to the world...

But completely known by the God who created him.

It's Just Me Lord, Nobody Special

And on that quiet night, beneath a dark sky, Timmy learned something he never forgot—that God doesn't miss a single lost lamb.

Not even the one sitting outside, singing softly into the dark.

He didn't understand what he felt that night.

Not fully.

It wasn't loud.

It wasn't dramatic.

Just a quiet stirring inside—like someone had seen him when no one else did.

Like God had pulled up a bench and sat beside him.

As if somebody, somewhere was covering him in prayer.

And maybe... somebody was.

Somebody like Grandma Taylor.

And even though nothing had changed on the outside...

Something had changed.

Because once you realize you're not invisible to God—

You start looking for Him in other places, too.

In songs.

In stories.

Even in silence.

Timmy didn't know it yet...

But sometimes, the moments that matter most come when you

feel stuck.

And the only way out...

Is to be rescued.

10 LET MY PEOPLE GO

There were a few unspoken rules at the Baptist church that Timmy grew up in.

Besides which verse of the song to stand on or sit on.

Don't talk during the sermon.

Don't run in the sanctuary.

And whatever you do—don't get up to go to the bathroom in the middle of preaching.

But when you're nine going on ten years old—sitting on a hard wooden pew in a room packed full of worn Bibles, stiff collars, and old folks fanning themselves with cardboard funeral-home fans stapled to tongue depressors—sometimes your bladder doesn't care about the rules.

It's Just Me Lord, Nobody Special

Timmy had tried to wait. He really had. He'd squirmed.

Crossed his legs. Tried thinking about dry deserts and

tumbleweeds.

But eventually, he whispered the dreaded words to Daddy.

"I gotta go."

Daddy gave him the look—the one that said, "You better

really have to."

Timmy nodded with urgency, clutching his stomach for dramatic

effect.

And with that, he slid off the pew and made the long,

humiliating journey to the front of the church.

See, the bathrooms weren't in the back like they were in

most churches. No sir. Not this one.

At this church, the only way to the bathroom was to walk all the

way to the front of the sanctuary—past the preacher, past the

pulpit, and through a little wooden door just to the right of the

platform.

He could feel every eye in the sanctuary latch onto him like

heat-seeking missiles.

Every step he took echoed louder than the last.

Clack. Clack. Clack.

The soles of his shoes suddenly sounded like tap shoes on a stage.

He even tried to walk softer, but that only made it worse— like a guilty whisper in a silent room.

When he finally reached the door, he grabbed the knob with sweaty fingers and slipped through it like he was escaping enemy territory.

A wave of cooler air hit him as the door shut behind him, and the sounds of the sanctuary faded.

The hallway stretched out in front of him—dimly lit, lined with Sunday school classrooms, and smelling faintly of old hymnals, mildew, and Pine-Sol. His footsteps on the linoleum floor sounded like a prison march.

At the very end of the hallway was the men's room—just a single door with a faded sign and a doorknob that had clearly seen better days.

Timmy stepped inside and sighed with relief.

The bathroom was tiny, the floor was cold, the light overhead flickered once before buzzing to life.

There was one toilet, one tiny sink with a stubborn faucet, and a warped mirror that made your face look wobbly around the edges.

He did his business quickly, washed his hands with pink industrial soap that smelled like chalk and regret, and wiped them on the rough paper towels that came out two at a time, whether you needed them or not.

Then he reached for the door to head back to his seat...
And the knob came off in his hand.

At first, he just blinked.
Stared at it like it had betrayed him.

The whole thing had slipped free, clean as could be—like it was never attached in the first place.
Only a stub of the shaft remained, poking out of the door like a broken bone.

Maybe he could just slide it back on?

He tried—gently at first. Then with a little more pressure.
But instead of catching...
clink.
The stub slipped through the hole and fell onto the linoleum in the hallway outside—along with the other half of the knob.

He gasped.

Now there was nothing left.

Just a square hole where the shaft used to be.

No way to grab it.

No way to turn it.

No way to get out.

The air got heavy.

The room suddenly felt smaller.

His pulse kicked up, thudding in his ears like a bass drum.

He backed up from the door like it was alive.

Then stepped forward again and tried jiggling the latch, ramming it with his shoulder, pressing his thumb into the square hole.

Nothing.

He was trapped.

Panic rushed in like a wave.

His throat tightened. His breathing turned short and shallow.

The walls crept in closer with every second.

He was claustrophobic, and this wasn't just a bathroom anymore.

It was a tomb with bad lighting and no escape.

What if nobody came?

What if the church service ended, and everyone just… forgot about him?

He could hear it in his mind—hymnals closing, footsteps fading, the sanctuary door creaking shut one last time.

What if they turned off the lights, locked the building, and drove away?

His heart pounded harder. His throat tightened.

The fear wasn't funny anymore.

It was real.

And it swallowed him whole.

And then it happened—pure instinct.

He screamed.

"HELP!"

His voice bounced off the tile like a cannon blast.

"HELP! I'M STUCK! I CAN'T GET OUT!"

He beat on the door with both fists. His hands stung. His voice cracked.

His whole body shook with fear, embarrassment, and frustration.

Out in the sanctuary, the preacher had stopped preaching mid-sentence.

You could've heard a pin drop.

Then came the shuffling. Footsteps. Quick and confused.

A few seconds later, the door burst open—two men stood there, wide-eyed, staring at the scene:

little Timmy Rimmer, sweaty, red-faced, breathless, and holding half of a doorknob like it was a weapon.

There was a long pause.

"Timmy?" one of them asked.

He nodded.

Couldn't speak.

They didn't laugh. Not yet.

But he knew they wanted to.

He stepped past them, out into the hallway. The cool air hit him again, but this time it didn't feel refreshing.

It felt like stage lights.

His shoes squeaked as he walked.

And when he opened the door back into the sanctuary... the sound returned.

It's Just Me Lord, Nobody Special

Coughs.

Sniffles.

Shuffling papers.

Quiet chuckles.

He didn't look left.

He didn't look right.

He just walked. Straight down the aisle.

And all those eyes?

They were still watching.

Except now, they weren't just watching.

They were grinning.

He made it back to the pew where Daddy sat, still facing forward like nothing had happened.

Timmy sat down beside him, heart pounding.

Elton didn't say a word. Didn't even glance his way.

But the damage was done.

He would forever be "the kid who got trapped in the bathroom during service."

It was supposed to be a sanctuary.

But that day, it felt more like a prison.

And if you had asked him what the preacher had been talking about before the screaming started?

He couldn't have told you.

But one phrase echoed in his head for the rest of the day:

Let my people go.

It wasn't just a line from the Bible that morning.

It was a cry from Timmy's heart.

A plea to be free—from fear, from ridicule, from everything that made him feel small.

He didn't know it yet,

but soon—he'd face a very different kind of fire.

And this one wouldn't come from a sermon.

11 BrUSH FirE

It was summer in Arkansas, and Timmy and Jessie had already spent the morning burning through their usual list of outdoor fun—shooting tin cans with their Red Ryder BB guns, digging intricate dirt roads for their Tonka dump trucks, and daring each other to run barefoot through the hidden sticker patch beneath the tall mimosa trees in the middle of the yard.

But as the sun climbed higher, the air grew thick and heavy—the kind of heat that made your skin sticky and your lungs tired.
The cicadas droned endlessly, their buzzing voices weaving through the humid air—a relentless warning that the hottest part

of the day had arrived. Even the breeze, when it came, was warm and carried the scent of dust and dry grass.

Their energy drained, and soon even their usual games lost their appeal.

They were bored.

The boys weren't allowed inside. They knew that. Barbara was in one of her "stay outside and play" moods, which meant the house was off-limits unless someone was actively bleeding.

"We're thirsty!" Jessie called through the screen door.

Barbara's answer was quick and firm. "Get a drink from the hose!"

The boys groaned in unison. Hose water was warm. It tasted like rubber and metal.

Jessie sighed. "Forget that. I'm getting water from inside." He darted toward the back door before Timmy could object.

The screen door creaked as he slipped inside, stepping into the kitchen. The air was cooler in here, carrying the faint scent of cornbread baking in the oven. He grabbed a glass from the dish rack, turned toward the sink—then he saw it.

A small box on the kitchen counter.

Jessie glanced over his shoulder. No one was watching.

His hand darted out, snatching up the tiny box. His heart pounded as he quickly slid it into his pocket. He turned on the faucet, letting the water rush into the glass, took a quick gulp, and left the half-full glass on the counter before slipping back outside.

Timmy was waiting.

"Where's the water?" Timmy asked, frowning at Jessie's empty hands.

Jessie grinned, pulling the box from his pocket. "Forget water. Look what I got."

Timmy's stomach dropped as he stared down. "What is it?"

Jessie smirked, tilting the box slightly—just enough for Timmy to see inside.

Matches.

Timmy's eyes widened. "You're gonna get us in trouble!"

Jessie shrugged, already thinking ahead. "Not if we're careful."

Timmy hesitated. He knew this was a bad idea. But he also knew something else—if he didn't go along, Jessie was going to do it anyway.

"Fine," he muttered. "But not here."

They couldn't stay in the yard. Too risky.

So, they snuck next door, crossing into the vacant lot where an old mobile home had once stood. Now, only a set of wooden steps, a concrete slab, and a rusted butane tank remained. The area was overgrown, knee-high wild sage grass swaying in the occasional breeze. The butane tank, its faded white paint now streaked with rust, sat eerily still—an old giant sleeping in the heat of the afternoon.

But the real danger wasn't the tank.

It was the grass—tall, dry, and brittle from weeks without rain. It hissed softly when the wind moved through it, almost as if whispering a warning.

Jessie struck the first match.

A tiny flame flickered to life, then disappeared beneath his shoe as he stomped it out.

Timmy hesitated, but then he tried it too.

It was harmless fun—or so they thought.

Strike.

Toss.

Stomp.

A small thrill each time, watching the flame dance for a second before it vanished beneath their feet.

But then—Jessie had an idea.

"Let's see who can wait the longest before stomping it out," he challenged, a grin spreading across his face.

Timmy hesitated. "I don't know…"

But Jessie had already struck another match.

He let it burn for a moment longer than before.

Then stomped.

Timmy followed suit, waiting just a second longer than usual before snuffing it out.

Then another.

Then another.

With each match, they got bolder.

They watched the tiny flames flicker, testing their limits—seeing just how long they could hold out before smashing their feet down.

A second longer.

Then two.

The heat curled at their ankles, teasing danger.

But they weren't scared.

Not yet.

Not until Jessie flicked a match—and the flame landed wrong.

It touched the sage grass instead of the dirt.

And before either of them could react—it spread.

Timmy's foot came down hard, but the fire had already jumped past his shoe.

Jessie tried to kick dirt over it, but the wind had other plans.

The smell of burning grass hit their noses—sharp and choking.

Flames shot through the dry grass like a living thing, growing taller, hotter, faster than they could think. The fire crackled with a terrifying hunger, its orange tongues licking greedily at the sky.

The heat hit them like an open oven door.

"FIRE! FIRE!"

They turned to run—but where? The fire was moving

toward the butane tank. The whole lot could explode.

Panic.

Barbara burst through the door, her eyes locking on the

flames in an instant.

"JERRY, GET OUT HERE—NOW!"

Jerry grabbed a broom and ran toward the fire, swinging

wildly, but it was no use. The flames swallowed the dry brush in

seconds, the heat searing against their faces.

Then—a sound.

A truck engine.

Elton. Just pulling up from a long day at work.

The pickup skidded into the driveway, gravel flying as he jumped

out and took in the disaster in one glance.

He grabbed the nearest hose—too short.

He muttered under his breath but didn't hesitate.

Without missing a beat, he yanked an old towel from the truck,

soaked it in a bucket, and started beating the fire with it.

Jerry swung the half-melted broom.

Barbara used her wet towel.

The battle was on.

It's Just Me Lord, Nobody Special

Smoke burned their lungs.

Ash swirled in the air.

And still—the fire fought back.

The butane tank loomed just feet away, and Elton's face hardened. He swung harder, his arms moving with everything he had. Barbara coughed, her eyes stung from the thick smoke, but she didn't stop.

Finally…

The flames weakened.

Then—died.

All that remained was blackened earth and a lingering haze of smoke.

Nobody spoke at first.

Elton turned slowly, his gaze landing on Timmy and Jessie. They knew exactly what was coming next.

The next sound Timmy heard was a familiar one—Elton's belt ripping through half a dozen belt loops with a sharp, snapping rhythm: thip-thip-thip-thip-thip-thip.

The sting was instant—but not as bad as the fear of what could have happened.

They had seen fire before.

But never like that.

Never that close.

Never so out of control.

By the time Barbara sent them to their room, their legs were sore, their lungs still heavy with smoke, and their hearts still hammering from the terror of watching flames race toward that butane tank.

The next morning, the lot was eerily silent.
Where there had once been golden grass, there was now only blackened earth, charred sticks, and the ghostly outline of their footprints leading away from the scorched field.

They never played with matches again.
In fact, it would be weeks before either of them played with anything at all.

And though the lesson burned deep, there was something else Timmy carried with him—something quieter, but just as lasting.
Because that night, as he lay in bed, still smelling the faint scent of smoke on his clothes, his thoughts drifted to someone else.

It's Just Me Lord, Nobody Special

Someone who never would have tolerated two boys being so reckless.

Someone whose patience was as steady as his hands—who could build things up just as easily as fire could burn them down.

His mind wandered to an old porch,

A rocking chair,

And a man who rarely spoke—because he didn't have to.

12 DADDY'S DADDY

Some men build houses. Some build legacies. Grandpa Rimmer did both.

Timmy didn't know much about his grandpa, Arthur Young Rimmer—but he sure knew that old rocking chair on the front porch.

Oh, that chair… the way it creaked back and forth, steady as the land it sat upon. It wasn't just a place to sit. It was his place. A place where time slowed down, where the worries of the world faded into the rhythm of the rockers against the concrete slab.

That porch—cool in the mornings, baking hot in the afternoons—was Grandpa's kingdom.

In that chair sat a man of quiet power. He didn't talk much.

He didn't have to.

His presence said everything.

Grandpa wore his overalls like armor, day in and day out.

His hands, rough and thick from decades of carpentry, bore the

marks of a man who had carved a life out of wood, sweat, and

willpower. When he wasn't whittling with his pocketknife, he

was dipping into his pouch of Red Man chewing tobacco. He'd

pick through it like a jeweler examining gems, tossing out what

didn't make the cut. And every now and then, he'd hold out a

piece—just to see if you were bold enough to take it.

Timmy was once.

Just once.

One chew, and that was enough to make a boy see stars.

Grandpa just chuckled, low and deep.

"Ain't for boys," he muttered, spitting clean off the porch

like he had perfect aim.

But there was something more to Grandpa Rimmer than his

tobacco or his rocking chair. There was a look in his eyes.

Timmy didn't understand it then, but he would one day. Those

eyes spoke of a love that was gone—a love for Grandma, the

woman who had once filled his days with joy. Timmy had never known her, but he felt her absence in the way Grandpa's gaze sometimes drifted—soft, unfocused—toward nothing in particular, like he was remembering something only he could see. It wasn't loud. It wasn't obvious. But it was there. Quiet. Steady. As sure as the creak of the chair beneath him.

Sometimes, Grandpa would take a slow walk around the yard. And when he did, Timmy would fall into step beside him, reaching up to grab hold of the hammer loop on his overalls. He didn't say anything. Neither did Grandpa.
They just walked.

Timmy's little legs would stretch to keep up, his hand gripping that loop like it connected him to something bigger.

And maybe it did.

Then there were the pigeons.

Every morning, those birds would gather in the driveway, waiting. Like clockwork. Grandpa would scatter cornbread crumbs for them—nothing fancy, just enough. He never talked to them. Never shooed them. Just fed them.
And somehow, they knew to come back.

It's Just Me Lord, Nobody Special

It was their ritual.

Quiet. Simple. Sacred.

Timmy would watch from the steps, the smell of tobacco hanging in the air, the morning sun cutting long shadows across the gravel, the pigeons cooing softly as they pecked at crumbs.

But then… one day, Grandpa didn't come out.

The rocking chair sat still.

The pigeons waited.

And when no one came—

They stopped coming too.

There's a kind of silence that settles in after someone leaves. It's not just quiet.

It's absence.

Timmy missed the sound of the blade on wood. Missed the creak of the rocker. Missed the scratchy scent of sawdust and the way Grandpa's silence filled the space with something that still felt like love.

He hadn't known how much noise Grandpa's stillness made—until it was gone.

One day, Grandpa took his last chew.

And just like that...

The porch grew quiet.

But even in that stillness—he lingered.

In the wood shavings.

In the pigeons.

In the quiet creak of an empty chair.

And in the boy who used to walk beside him, holding on for dear life to that old hammer loop.

Timmy carried that quiet strength with him—even into the smallest moments.

Because sometimes, it was in those everyday things—like folding towels or helping with laundry—that grandpa's steadiness showed up again.

And one day, while trying to be helpful...

Timmy learned the hard way that not all lessons come from a rocking chair.

13 HOLY ROLLERS

One of Timmy's hardest lessons came later—at the old white house on the road with tar and pea gravel, there were no shiny appliances or modern conveniences. Barbara didn't have a clothes dryer—or even a washing machine, like a lot of folks had by the late '70s. What she did have was a white porcelain wringer washer, parked on a patch of grass just outside the back door, flanked by two galvanized rinse tubs standing on spindly metal legs. It looked more like something out of a museum than something that still washed clothes.

But it worked.

And on warm days, Barbara would haul the dirty laundry outside and fire it up. The sound of birds chirping in the trees mixed with the occasional cluck of a chicken drifting over from the nearby coop. Dogs barked lazily in the distance, stirred only by rabbits rustling through the brush or a passing car on the nearby gravel road.

The wringer washer didn't have a proper drain hose—just a short black one that barely reached the ground. Soapy water poured out in spurts, soaking the grass around the base of the machine and turning the yard into a mushy patch of earth that squished beneath your feet. A cloud of white suds pooled around the washer, bubbling slightly with each new cycle.

On this particular day, the sun was high and hot, baking the ground under Timmy's bare feet as he trotted around the side of the house to the backyard. He'd just been in the front yard, tying sewing thread to the back leg of a June bug—a summertime tradition among country kids—and flying it around like a tiny green kite. It buzzed and spun in dizzy circles above him, shimmering metallic green in the sunlight, its wings flapping like it couldn't decide whether to escape or enjoy the ride.

But the second he heard the rhythmic whir of the washer, Timmy dropped the thread and ran around back to see if Barbara might let him help.

The air smelled of laundry soap, with a hint of Clorox bleach. Barbara was already halfway through the wash, her hands dipping clothes into the soapy basin and feeding them through the wringer one by one. The suds clung to her wrists, and she wiped her forearms with a dishrag tucked into her waistband.

Timmy had always been fascinated by the wringer—two rubber rollers set close together at the top of the machine. When powered on, they turned slowly, squeezing water from each piece of clothing as it passed through.

It wasn't that she didn't want help—it was that she didn't want to deal with accidents.

"You better keep your fingers back," she said without looking at him, her tone more warning than warm. "That thing'll take your hand off if you ain't careful."

Timmy nodded and watched closely, mesmerized as a wet pair of jeans was fed into the rollers and came out the other side flat and nearly dry.

"Can I do that?" he asked.

Barbara paused, glancing over at the basket of clothes waiting to be pinned to the line. After a moment, she stepped back.

"Fine," she said. "But be careful."

Timmy's heart raced as he stepped forward. He grabbed a T-shirt from the wash tub and fed the corner gently into the rollers. The machine took hold, pulling the shirt through slowly. It worked just like he'd seen.

One more piece of clothing. One more pass through the rollers.

Barbara moved toward the clothesline, basket in hand, wooden clothespins dangling from the hem of her shirt. The line stretched between two rusty T-posts, already sagging under the weight of damp shirts and faded jeans fluttering in the breeze. The air was rich with the smell of soap, sunshine, and the faint scent of chickens scratching in the dirt nearby.

Timmy felt proud. He was doing it. Helping. Contributing. But then—he reached for the next item, a heavy towel, and his hand slipped.

It happened in an instant.
The towel caught in the rollers—and so did Timmy's fingers. Before he could react, the machine pulled his hand in—then his wrist—then his forearm—all the way up to his elbow.

"Awwwwww!" he screamed. "Help! It's got me!"

The wringer didn't care. It kept turning, dragging him in tighter. His skin pressed against the rubber rollers, hot and pinched. Tears filled his eyes. Panic rose in his chest.

Barbara turned, dropped her basket, and rushed over. "Oh Lord," she muttered, yanking the plug from the wall. The machine gave a slow hum and stopped. The rollers froze, but Timmy's arm was still stuck, wedged between the unforgiving rubber grips.

Barbara's hands were shaking as she tried to reverse the tension. She turned the release lever, and slowly—painfully—the rollers gave way just enough for Timmy to pull his arm free.

He stumbled back, holding his elbow, the imprint of the rollers clearly marked in his skin. It throbbed, but it wasn't broken. Just bruised.

"You alright?" Barbara asked, her voice tight.

Timmy nodded, still catching his breath.

She didn't say another word—just went back to the line.

The breeze picked up as Barbara pinned a towel to the line, and droplets of water flung off the corner as it flapped in the wind. Timmy stood off to the side, cradling his arm and watching her work.

She never looked back at him. Never asked if he was really okay. Maybe she didn't know what to say—or maybe in their house, pain was something you handled alone. You didn't cry, and you didn't expect comfort. You just got out of the way and tried not to make trouble.

And maybe—just maybe—that rule applied more to him than anyone else.

And Timmy?

He didn't go near that wringer again for a long time.

But even now, decades later, he can still feel the rubber pressing into his skin. He can still hear the hum of the motor, the clatter of the laundry basket hitting the ground, the flap of wet jeans on the clothesline, and the birds calling in the trees above. He can still feel the soaked ground squish under his toes. He can still see that June bug spiraling on its thread like a helicopter gone haywire.

It wasn't just a washing machine.

It was a memory burned into him as clearly as the bruises that once wrapped around his arm.

Family meant everything. And in Timmy's world, family always had a way of bringing warmth, laughter, and unforgettable memories.

14 AUNT OPAL

There was more than one way to get to Aunt Opal's house from their home on Military Road. The surest way—the one most of the family took—was to turn left at the end of the driveway, follow the road just before you reached the rickety one-lane bridge that spanned the creek, then take another left. From there, it was a steady mile-long climb up the dirt road, where the hill gradually revealed the small white house at the top—the place where Aunt Opal and Uncle Howard lived.

That was the easy way.

But easy wasn't always the fun way.

For an adventurous boy like Timmy, there was a shortcut. A path that required squeezing through the barbed wire fence at the edge of the yard, cutting across the neighbor's pasture, dodging cow patties, and hoping—praying—the old bull wasn't around. That shortcut shaved a good bit of time off the trip—but it came at a cost.

A painful cost.

Because the thing about barbed wire?

It bites.

Timmy had learned to pull up on the top strand while pushing down on the middle one, just enough to shimmy through. He had done it a dozen times before. Maybe a hundred. But this time?

This time, he wasn't quite careful enough.

As he slid through the gap, one of the rusted barbs snagged his stomach, and before he could jerk away, it ripped through his skin—a sharp, searing pain that made him suck in his breath.

He looked down.

A thin red line stretched across his belly, about eight inches long, already beginning to bead with blood.

He wiped at it, wincing as the sting flared up again. But there was no time to worry about that now. He had a shortcut to finish, a pasture to cross, and an aunt waiting at the top of the hill—probably with something fresh out of the oven.

So, with one last glance at the wound, he ignored the pain and kept going.
Because a little blood never stopped an adventure.

But taking the pasture route also meant missing out on the bridge—and missing out on the bridge meant missing out on one of the greatest pastimes a country boy could have: flipping over rocks in the shallow water, searching for crawdads. More than once, a "quick trip" to Aunt Opal's turned into an afternoon adventure, hands and knees muddy from digging, pockets filled with wiggling trophies and shiny rocks that never quite made it home.

But no matter how you got there, you always knew when you had arrived.
Long before the house came into view, the air itself told you.

First, there was the scent of sawdust. Uncle Howard was a carpenter, just like his daddy before him, and the carport wasn't just for parking cars. It was his workshop—a place where hammers rang against nails and fresh-cut lumber perfumed the air. Sawdust settled into every crack and crevice, and no matter how many times he swept, it was never truly gone. It clung to his work boots, settled in the folds of his overalls, and floated in the air like a fine dusting of golden snow. To Timmy, the scent of sawdust was as much a part of Aunt Opal's house as the walls themselves.

But as soon as you stepped past the carport and up the stairs, the scent shifted.

Because inside, Aunt Opal was cooking.

And if Aunt Opal was cooking, you were eating.

It wasn't a question. It wasn't an offer. It was a fact.

It didn't matter if you had just finished breakfast or if you swore you weren't hungry. Aunt Opal had a way of putting a plate in front of you before you could protest. And if you were foolish enough to claim you weren't hungry, she'd just smile and say, "Well, just in case," before piling your plate full anyway.

But for all the delicious meals, the warm biscuits, and the kitchen full of laughter, it wasn't the food that fascinated Timmy the most about Aunt Opal's house.

The real magic was just outside the sliding back door.

Nestled in the backyard, no more than ten feet across and maybe two feet deep, was a goldfish pond. A perfect little concrete circle, bordered by a narrow sidewalk, filled with shimmering golden fish that darted beneath the lily pads at the slightest movement. To an adult, it was a simple thing—just a backyard pond.

But to a nine-year-old boy?

It was magnificent.

Timmy could stand there for ages, inching forward as carefully as possible, hoping to catch a glimpse of the fish before they vanished into the shadows.

"Don't get too close!" someone would always call out. "You might fall in!"

Which, of course, only made Timmy want to inch closer.

Maybe—just maybe—if he got close enough, accidentally on purpose, he would fall in.

And maybe—just maybe—he'd finally catch one of those little fish in his bare hands.

But time had a way of slipping by too fast at Aunt Opal's house, and before long, it was time to head home.

If you were on foot, the trip back was easy.

But if you had ridden your bike up that hill?

Well, that was another story entirely.

It's Just Me Lord, Nobody Special

Going up was slow, grueling work—the kind that made your legs ache and your lungs burn.

But coming down?

Coming down meant speed.

Meant wind in your face.

Meant gripping the long handlebars of a Schwinn bicycle, white-knuckled and grinning, as the dirt road blurred beneath you.

Coming down also meant—you'd better watch out for the rocks.

The little ones weren't a problem.

But the big ones?

The big ones had a way of leaping right in front of your tire at the worst possible moment.

One second, Timmy was king of the world—the breeze whipping through his hair, the ground rushing by beneath him as he raced downhill, faster and faster, with that weightless, exhilarating feeling that only comes when you're young and invincible.

The next—His bike stopped.

But Timmy did not.

The front tire slammed into a rock the size of a softball, jerking the handlebars sideways. In an instant, he was airborne, flipping head over heels before landing—hard—into the briar-lined ditch.

His knees? Skinned.

His elbows? Scraped.

His pride? Dented.

The gravel and thorns left their mark, a stinging souvenir of the day's adventure. Blood mixed with dirt, and for a moment, he just lay there, catching his breath, staring up at the sky.

But country boys didn't cry over a little blood and dirt.

No sir.

So Timmy did what any good country boy would do.

He picked himself up.

He brushed himself off.

And he got right back on that bike.

Aunt Opal and Uncle Howard are long gone now, but the memories remain—anchored in the scent of sawdust, the flash of goldfish darting beneath lily pads, and the thrill of a bike ride down a dusty Arkansas hill.

It's Just Me Lord, Nobody Special

Those bike rides back from Aunt Opal's were some of
Timmy's earliest lessons in risk and reward—how a little danger
could make a memory last forever. But more often than not, it
wasn't adventure that called him home. It was Barbara's voice
from the kitchen, yelling through the screen door for sugar, or
flour, or something she forgot on her last trip into town. The
wildness of the day faded fast when supper was on the stove.
And in their house, supper came from wherever wild things still
grew.

15 WHERE THE WILD THINGS ARE

Out in the middle of nowhere, supper didn't come from a store—not all of it, anyway.

It came from the dirt, the garden, and whatever happened to be growing wild that week.

In the front yard, wild onions shot up through the grass like little green straws. Jessie loved them. He would pluck them straight from the ground, knock off the extra clumps of mud, and bite down like he was eating green licorice.

His breath could clear a room, but he didn't care. Most afternoons, he could be found pushing his big yellow Tonka dump truck around the front yard, the bed piled high with wild onions like he was running a roadside stand.

Not far from there, across the yard and around the garden fence, poke salad grew in thick patches. Timmy didn't think much about how dangerous it could be if it wasn't cooked right—he just knew Barbara boiled it more than once before it ever hit the skillet. The scent was strong and earthy, especially once she dropped in the bacon grease and stirred in scrambled eggs with the edge of a wooden spoon.

It didn't smell good, exactly.

But it smelled like home.

By late afternoon, the whole house felt like a stove. The kitchen windows were cracked open, and the box fan rattled by the screen door, blowing the heat back outside.

Timmy would be out in the yard when Barbara's voice rang out like a dinner bell:

"Timmy! Pick a couple of tomatoes from the garden for supper!"

He'd head toward the vines barefoot, careful not to step on a yellow jacket nest, his feet green from walking around in the grass without shoes.

The tomatoes were still warm from the sun, and every now and then, a praying mantis would be clinging to the vine, swaying like he owned the place. Timmy would freeze, lock eyes with it, and ease his hand around to the other side of the plant.

He'd wipe the tomatoes on his shirt and bring them inside like prize eggs.

Inside, the pressure cooker on the stove was already working on a pot of brown beans. The metal spindle on top danced back and forth, letting out a sharp, steady rhythm—

tst… tst… tst… tst… tst… tst…

—filling the kitchen.

Nestled down in the pot was a ham bone, left over from last week's supper, giving the beans their flavor and soul. Barbara had a way of filling the table, even when the cabinets looked bare: brown beans, fried potatoes, sliced tomatoes still warm from the vine. Poke salad with scrambled eggs and a hint of bacon. And always—always—some kind of meat. Pork chops. Fried chicken. Meatloaf stretched with saltines and ketchup.

She had to cook big, because there were five mouths to feed—

And none of them went to bed hungry.

And of course, there was cornbread.

There was always cornbread.

It's Just Me Lord, Nobody Special

Baked in a cast-iron skillet, golden on the edges and soft in the middle.

Later in life, Barbara handed that job over to Timmy. But at 9 years old, he only watched, standing near the oven with his mouth watering.

In the middle of the dark wood table—surrounded by floral-upholstered chairs—sat a big red ceramic strawberry cookie jar. It didn't hold much more than bills, receipts, and a few random keys that Elton more than likely left in his pocket when he came home from work, but it was always there—like part of the family.

And waiting on that table, alongside all that food, was a gallon-sized glass pickle jar filled with Southern sweet tea—brewed strong, served cold, and sweetened with a cup and a half of sugar. The kind of tea that made your teeth hurt...
But you poured a second glass anyway.

Sometimes, supper needed help.
Barbara would open the cabinet, realize they were out of sugar, or tea bags, or a scoop of flour, and she'd call out again—
"Timmy! Ride your bike up to Opal's and borrow some!"

He'd hop on the Schwinn—banana seat and all—pedal through the gravel, and make the familiar trip up the road. Aunt Opal never minded. She'd hand him a paper sack with whatever they needed—sometimes with a smile, sometimes with a warning not to spill it. And before heading home, Timmy would always sneak around back to steal a quick look at her goldfish pond.

Back home, the pressure cooker still hissed.

Jessie was probably still chewing on his harvest.

Jerry was nearly done setting the table.

And out past the fence line, just as the sun dipped behind the trees, the whippoorwills began to sing—

A slow, lonesome call that meant the day was almost done.

This was where the wild things were—

Not in the woods.

Not in some far-off place.

But right here in the yard, the garden, the kitchen, and the quiet minutes before Daddy's truck rolled down the driveway.

Timmy didn't know it then, but those simple suppers—stitched together from what they could gather—would become the kind of memories that stuck like the smell of fried potatoes in his shirt.

Even now, if he heard that soft rhythmic hiss—

tst... tst... tst... tst... tst... tst...

He'd know exactly what time it was.

Supper time.

And Daddy's almost home.

16 WHere We're GOING, We DON'T NEED SeaTBeLTS

Back in the 1970s, before seatbelt laws and safety regulations took the fun out of everything, riding in the back of a pickup truck wasn't just normal—it was a rite of passage.

Nobody worried about helmets or harnesses. You just climbed in, held on tight, and hoped Daddy missed the biggest potholes.

For Timmy, Jerry, and Jessie, the back of Daddy's truck was more than just transportation—It was freedom, thrill, and sometimes, punishment all rolled into one.

It's Just Me Lord, Nobody Special

During the day, it was the best seat in the house. The boys would stand tall, gripping the back of the cab as the world flew past at 55 miles per hour—wind in their faces, shirts flapping, laughter carried off behind them. If Daddy hit the hills just right, they'd feel their stomachs drop, their feet lifting for a second before landing back on the metal bed with a satisfying thud.

But when the sun went down, everything changed.

Some nights, Daddy would load the boys up and head out to visit friends. It never mattered how far away they lived— visiting meant staying for hours. While the grown-ups gathered inside to play spades, sipping on Coke and crunching chips between card slaps and laughter, the kids made the yard their own.

Chicken fights were the game of choice. One boy would hop on the shoulders of another, trying to knock the other team down while wobbling in the soft dirt. Grass stains, scraped knees, and belly laughs were the price of victory—and nobody minded paying.

But when Daddy finally said, "Alright, let's load up," The fun ended cold—literally.

16 Where We're Going, We Don't Need Seatbelts

There weren't enough seats in the cab for everyone. So while Barbara climbed in up front and Daddy took the wheel, three boys scrambled into the truck bed, bracing themselves against the chill. Timmy, Jerry, and Jessie would huddle near the cab, trying to block the wind, their breath fogging in the cold night air.

That is—two of them would.
Because somehow, Jessie always managed to sneak into the front seat.

He'd whine about being tired or cold, slump his shoulders just right, maybe even fake a shiver or two. Barbara would sigh, shake her head, and open the door. "Get in," she said.

And in he'd go, flashing that smug little grin—while Timmy and Jerry gritted their teeth and braced for the ride.

There were certain spots on the ride home they always knew were coming.
Like the railroad crossing.

If a train passed, it was a blessing in disguise. Daddy would have to stop, and the wind would finally pause for a few precious moments. Jerry and Timmy would stand up and lean over the cab, counting the train cars as they rumbled past—clank, clank, clank—one after another.

No safety gates came down to block the road back then. Just a flicker of red in the darkness—a flare dropped by the engineer to warn of the passing train. Smoke curled upward into the cool night sky as the caboose finally brought up the rear.

And then—just like that—the engine roared to life again, and the truck took off down the road.

Jerry would yank Timmy back down into the truck bed, and they'd brace themselves—because the second that truck started moving again, the cold came roaring back.

And the real torture kicked in:

The hills.

What felt like a rollercoaster during the day turned into pure misery at night. As the truck dipped down into one of the big hills, the cold air rushed in harder, sharper—cutting straight through their jackets and clothes like knives of winter.

They'd crouch lower, faces tucked into their shirts, arms folded tight against their chests.

And the bumps?

They were brutal.

The metal bed of the truck bounced and rattled, jarring their backs and freezing their bones.

Jerry had a game he liked to play to distract himself—he'd lie flat on his back, eyes closed, and try to guess where they were by the feel of the road beneath them.

"That was the second bridge," he'd mutter, eyes still shut.

Sharp curve?

Almost home.

Big hill?

Time to brace.

It wasn't just a ride—It was survival.

But somehow, they made it.

As soon as Daddy pulled into the driveway, the truck bed exploded with movement. Timmy and Jerry scrambled out, legs stiff, hands numb, racing for the front door like it was the finish line of a marathon.

The heater inside the house roared to life, and they'd stand in front of it, arms stretched wide, rubbing their hands together and trying to feel their fingers again.

It was a cold that didn't just sting your skin—It stayed with you, burrowing deep.

And every single time, Timmy made the same vow:

"Next time, I'm getting that front seat."

But even he knew the truth.

Jessie would always find a way in.

And Timmy?

He'd always be riding in the back.

Those long rides home in the back of Daddy's truck—huddled up against the cold, wind in their faces, Jessie hogging the front seat as usual—weren't just about getting from one place to another.

They were about belonging.

About being part of something.

And if there was ever a place that made Timmy feel like he belonged, it was Aunt Mary Bell's house.

Because on Sundays, the whole family showed up.

And when Aunt Mary Bell was cooking?

You didn't need an invitation.

You just needed to show up hungry...

17 AUNT MARY BELL

It was a simpler time in Arkansas in the 1970s—a time when the world slowed down on Sundays. There was a rhythm to the day, a comforting cadence that never seemed to change, at least not for Timmy. It started with the sweet chime of church bells, the rustling of Bible pages in Sunday School, and the preacher's voice rising and falling like the Arkansas hills. He loved the stories, the songs, and the warmth of being at church.

But if Timmy was being honest, there was one thing he looked forward to more than the sermon—Sunday dinner at Aunt Mary Bell's.

While Timmy and his family were at Sunday School, learning about David and Goliath or Jonah and the whale,

Aunt Mary Bell—Elton's older sister—was at home, busy in the kitchen, crafting a meal that could make angels sigh. Every week, she performed this delicious ritual, filling her house with a rich, mouthwatering aroma.

The menu never changed, and it didn't need to. It was the kind of meal you could smell from the yard—the kind that pulled you in like a magnet: crispy fried chicken, golden and seasoned just right; buttery mashed potatoes, smooth enough to make you weep; and then there were the baked beans—rich, smoky, sweet, and absolutely unforgettable. No one knew exactly what went into them. Some swore it was brown sugar. Others said molasses. But the truth? Aunt Mary Bell never told. And now, that secret's gone with her.

By the time the last hymn was sung and the final "Amen" echoed through the sanctuary, Timmy was practically bouncing in his seat. His stomach growled in anticipation as the family loaded into the car and made their way down the familiar backroads toward Mary Bell's house.

And they weren't the only ones. The driveway and front yard were always full—cousins, aunts, uncles, and friends—all drawn by the unmistakable aroma of home-cooked magic. The windows fogged from the heat inside, the air thick with the smell of fried chicken and fresh-baked cornbread, and the laughter of family spilled out across the yard.

But the kids? They didn't hang around waiting. No, they were sent outside, where freedom waited under an open sky. There were no phones or tablets—just energy, imagination, and an open yard that became a kingdom.

Hide and seek. Freeze tag. Red Rover. Swing the Statue. They played them all. And if the yard ever felt too small, there was always the billboard—a massive sign standing tall beside the highway. To the adults, it was dangerous. To the kids, it was a grand adventure. They climbed it, sat at the top, and looked out like kings.

The adults hollered, "Y'all get down from there before you break your necks!"
But of course, that only made it more exciting.

Then came the call they'd all been waiting for:
"Kids, come eat!"

They barreled through the door, breathless and sweaty, taking their places at the worn, green table. No fresh plates—just whatever the adults had used. And no one cared. Timmy's eyes locked on to the lone remaining chicken leg and a heaping scoop of those legendary baked beans. He ate like only a boy could—fueled by play and church and anticipation.

But the best part? The grand finale?
It sat just four feet away, perched atop the counter like a chocolate crown.

Aunt Mary Bell's Mississippi Mud Cake.

A brownie-based masterpiece, thick and fudgy, topped with gooey marshmallows and smothered in a warm, rich layer of chocolate icing. If Heaven has a dessert table, this cake will be front and center. And Timmy made sure to savor every bite.

While the kids ran back outside, bellies full and laughter rising once again, the adults gathered around the kitchen table for their own kind of fun—a game of Skit Skat. All it took was fifteen cents and a little bit of luck. Nickels and dimes clinked onto the table, the room filled with teasing, jokes, and friendly competition.

No one got rich—not with money anyway.
But in that little house, wrapped in the smells of dinner and the sounds of family, they were the wealthiest people in the world.

And as the sun slipped down behind the trees and the last car rumbled away, Timmy climbed into the backseat—his stomach full, his heart fuller. He smiled as he closed his eyes, already dreaming about next Sunday.

Aunt Mary Bell may no longer be here.

But her legacy?

It's served up fresh in the hearts of those who sat at her table, played in her yard, and tasted the kind of love that only comes in the form of fried chicken, baked beans, and a slice of Mississippi Mud Cake.

Sundays at Aunt Mary Bell's were all about full bellies, full hearts, and the kind of joy that came from being surrounded by people who loved you—even if they showed it by hollering across the room or sneaking the last roll when you weren't looking.

But not every day was filled with sweet tea and Skit Skat.

Some days... were marked by scraped knees, bad ideas, and one very thin line between fun and trouble.

And Timmy?

Well, he was about to cross it.

18 THIN LINE, BIG TROUBLE

Summers in rural Arkansas were made for adventure—long, hot days that smelled like honeysuckle and sunbaked gravel.

And for two boys—Timmy and his stepbrother Jessie—that meant one thing: speed.

The road in front of their house wasn't paved with smooth asphalt, no gentle rolling slopes—just a stretch of tar and pea gravel, shimmering under the brutal Arkansas sun, and a hill so steep it felt like the edge of a roller coaster.

It was the perfect place for a good old-fashioned race.

It's Just Me Lord, Nobody Special

Timmy and Jessie didn't settle for casual bike riding. Oh no.

They were daredevils, chasing the thrill, pushing their limits,

defying the laws of physics and common sense.

But today?

Today, they needed something more.

A real race deserved a real finish line.

And that's where things started to go terribly, terribly wrong.

Timmy searched for something to mark the finish—

something that would make it official.

No ribbon. No rope. No problem.

Because inside the carport, sitting forgotten near Daddy's

workbench, was a spool of fishing line—thin as spider silk and

just as invisible in the midday sun.

He grabbed the spool, hurried to the end of the road, and

stretched it tight across the narrow two-lane. One end tied to the

mailbox, the other wrapped around his hand like a lasso. He

tugged it, testing the tension. It was perfect.

Jessie, oblivious to the impending disaster, climbed the hill,

gripping the long handlebars of his Schwinn bicycle. The

afternoon sun gleamed off its chrome fenders as he stood to

pedal, determination etched on his face. A baseball card, taped to the frame, smacked against the spokes with every turn of the wheel—roaring like a motorcycle, at least in his imagination.

The plan was simple.

Timmy would hold the line. Jessie would speed toward it.

And when he hit the finish line?

Sweet, undeniable victory.

Jessie reached the top of the hill.

Timmy held his breath.

The Schwinn creaked slightly as he shifted his weight, lining up for launch.

Then—it began.

Jessie pushed off, his feet pumping, tires spitting gravel as he gained speed.

Faster.

Faster.

The wind whipped against his face, stinging his eyes, tearing at his shirt. The world blurred past him. He imagined himself as Evel Knievel, fearless, unstoppable, destined for greatness.

He was going to win.

He was flying.

And then—WHAM.

It's Just Me Lord, Nobody Special

The fishing line pushed tight against his throat.

For half a second, it stretched—then snapped back like a slingshot.

His bike wobbled violently, the front tire skidding in the gravel. His arms flailed, desperate to regain balance.

For a split second, he thought he might save it.

Then—gravity had other plans.

His front wheel locked up.

His body kept going.

The world flipped upside down.

And then he was airborne.

Jessie hit the ground like a sack of potatoes, rolling, tumbling, arms and legs flailing in all directions. The sound of the bicycle scraping against gravel filled the air.

Then—silence.

Timmy's victory grin vanished.

Uh-oh.

Jessie lay on his back, staring at the trees cascading overhead, blinking in confusion. His hands shot to his throat, feeling for damage. A thin, angry red welt stretched across his skin.

And then, after a single gasping breath—

"AAAAAHHHH!"

Jessie let out a scream that could be heard in the next county.

Timmy's stomach dropped into his shoes.

This was bad.

And then—it got worse.

The screen door SLAMMED open.

Timmy knew that sound well.

Barbara had heard the commotion.

And when Barbara heard a commotion, it meant one thing:

Somebody was about to get it.

Timmy's feet twitched—his body screaming at him to RUN.

But before he could, a shadow stretched across the ground like an executioner's blade.

Timmy looked up.

Barbara stormed toward the willow tree, her nostrils flaring, her eyes sharp and unblinking.

The ground crunched beneath her feet with the weight of judgment.

It's Just Me Lord, Nobody Special

She reached for a branch, fingers wrapping around a long, thick switch.

She gave it a swift snap against her palm, testing its bite.

Timmy swallowed hard.

He had made a terrible mistake.

Jessie, never one to waste an opportunity, clutched his throat dramatically, gasping for air like he was on his deathbed. "Timmy—tried—to—kill—me!" Jessie moaned.

Timmy's mouth fell open. "I DID NOT!"

Barbara wasn't interested in negotiations.

In her right hand, the willow switch whistled through the air like a bullwhip.

His soul left his body.

Before Timmy could run—before he could even breathe— Barbara had him by the arm.

There was no escape.

What happened next was a blur of pain and regret.

By the time it was over, Timmy wasn't sure what hurt worse—his backside or his pride.

Barbara didn't even let him speak. Just pointed to the corner and walked off. So there he stood—arms folded, backside burning, eyes doing their best not to cry.

The great race?

A disaster.

The finish line?

Not worth it.

All he got for trying to have a little fun was a scolding. No praise. No "good job." Just a hard lesson he didn't ask for. He shifted from foot to foot, huffed through his nose, and muttered under his breath—"This is stupid."

And from the kitchen:

"What did you just say?"

Timmy learned that day that even the thinnest line—nearly invisible—can pack a punch when crossed the wrong way.

Sometimes, the line between fun and trouble is as thin as a strand of fishing line.

But not every line was meant to trip you up.

Some lines led to piles of presents, and the wide-eyed wonder of Christmas morning…

It's Just Me Lord, Nobody Special

Where the only thing sharper than a switch was the excitement in the air.

Because when you're a kid, Christmas isn't just a holiday. It's magic.

19 WONDERFUL, MAGICAL, NO FUSS, VERY BEST CHRISTMAS

There are plenty of things that make a young boy ask questions, but for Timmy, one mystery stood out above the rest.

It was Christmas—his favorite time of the year.

A season of joy, peace, and wonder.

And the thing that filled him with the most wonder was how different the city Santa Claus was from the country Santa Claus.

His cousins, Renee and Angie, had told him all about their Christmas mornings.

It's Just Me Lord, Nobody Special

They'd wake up to find their gifts neatly wrapped in shiny red and green paper, tied with ribbons and bows, waiting under the tree.

But at Timmy's house?

Things were... different.

Santa must have been in more of a hurry out in the country because he never bothered with wrapping paper.

Instead, he left three unwrapped piles of gifts next to the tree.

No names. No labels.

Just stacks of toys, one for each of the three brothers.

Timmy had tried to make sense of it all.

"How do you always know which pile is mine?" he had asked once.

Barbara didn't even hesitate.

"Santa tells us," she said matter-of-factly.

That answer didn't sit right with Timmy. Why did Santa have time to whisper secrets to his parents but couldn't spare a minute to wrap their presents?

It just didn't add up.

But there was no time to dwell on mysteries—Christmas morning was here.

Just as the first light of dawn touched the sky, Timmy's eyes popped open. His heart pounded with excitement.

Had Santa come?

Was it really Christmas morning?

He kicked off his electric blanket, barely feeling the chill in the air, and bolted off the top of his bunkbed.

The floor was icy beneath his bare feet, the kind of cold that made your teeth chatter, but he didn't care.

He tore through the house like a rocket, his tighty-whities and pajama top the only things between him and the freezing air.

The moment he stepped into the living room, Christmas hit all five senses at once.

Elton had already stoked the fire in their brand-new wood-burning stove, and the room was beginning to hum with a slow, toasty warmth.

The scent of burning oak filled the air, thick and smoky, blending with the sugary sweetness of chocolate-covered cherries sitting open on the coffee table.

It's Just Me Lord, Nobody Special

In the corner of the room stood their aluminum Christmas tree, glowing in all its tinsel glory.

It shimmered under the rotating color wheel on the floor beside it—fading from red to green to blue to gold every few seconds.

The silvery branches sparkled like icicles, each one carefully separated by stiff paper when they'd pulled them from the box the week before.

Plastic ornaments dangled from the limbs—some round and shiny, others shaped like bells or stars, their surfaces reflecting Timmy's wide-eyed face in distorted little swirls.

An angel rested crookedly on top; one wing bent from years of being crammed back into the same dusty box.

Timmy skidded to a stop on the red rug in front of the wood stove, his knees landing with a soft thud.

He sucked in a breath.

There they were.

Three unwrapped piles of toys, each one arranged neatly beside the tree.

His eyes darted from one to the next, scanning for clues.

And this year?

He didn't need anyone to tell him which one was his.

Sitting right on top of the middle stack was exactly what he had asked for.

A microscope.

The blue hard-shell case with the black handle gleamed in the glow of the color wheel as it slowly turned, casting hues of yellow and blue across the tree, the walls, and the presents below.

Mrs. Graves, his fifth-grade teacher, had been teaching them about germs.

She had let the class look through a real microscope at school, and Timmy had been awe-struck by the hidden world beneath the lens.

So when he saw the blue case, he knew—without a doubt—this pile was his.

He dropped to his knees, flipping the latches open with a satisfying click, and opened the lid to reveal the sleek microscope inside.

It was heavier than he expected, cool to the touch, and nestled in a molded bed of durable plastic.

It's Just Me Lord, Nobody Special

For a few moments, he forgot about everything else.

Forgot about his brothers tearing into their gifts—the ripping of cardboard, the crinkle of plastic packaging, the high-pitched squeals of discovery.

Forgot about the wooden sled leaning against the wall behind the tree—a shared gift from Santa with red metal runners, its wood slats sanded smooth and polished, ready for the nearest hill.

Forgot about the *Telstar Video Game Console* that Jerry was most excited about, even though it was technically their second shared gift that year.

Forgot about the *Digital Derby Handheld Racing Game* just inches from his knee.

He paid no attention to Jessie's brand-new Dallas Cowboy football helmet, its silver surface gleaming with promise.

The world had just shrunk down to the size of a slide beneath a lens.

The next few days were a blur of tiny discoveries.

A drop of water.

A strand of hair.

A speck of dirt.

He even put a booger under the lens—purely in the name of science, of course.

There were other treasures that year—a Concentration board game with clacking tiles, a Mickey Mouse Club Light Up Drawing Desk that buzzed softly when turned on, and his very first Holy Bible.

It was brand new, with a colorful cover showing Jesus sitting beneath a tree, surrounded by smiling children. The sky, soft blue behind them, and the grass beneath His feet looked almost real. A shiny gold cross—actually the zipper pull—hung on the upper corner.

Timmy ran his fingers over it before unzipping it slowly, the sound crisp, clean, and full of promise.

The pages inside were thin and bright white, edged in gold, and the red letters stood out like rubies on snow.

And, of course, the box of chocolate-covered cherries. His daddy's favorite.

There was one rule in the house when it came to chocolate-covered cherries:

If you took a bite, you had to finish it.

It's Just Me Lord, Nobody Special

No biting the chocolate, sucking out the filling, and leaving the rest.

Daddy wouldn't stand for it.

But there was something else in the room that Christmas morning.

Something that no one thought much about at the time.

A red rug.

It sat just in front of the wood-burning stove, spreading warmth across the floor where they had all gathered to open gifts.

Timmy's bare knees had pressed into it as he peered through his microscope, lost in the thrill of discovery.

In just eight days, that same rug would be wrapped around him—not for warmth, but for survival.

Because eight days after Christmas…

Things would get really heated.

20 Trial By Fire

It was January 2, 1979—just another winter evening in rural Arkansas.

The day was done, and the family sat around the kitchen table—just as they did every night. The steady clink of forks filled the silence between words.

Barbara was fussing at Timmy for not bringing his books home from school.

"You think you're gonna learn anything by leaving all your work in your desk?" she snapped.

Timmy didn't answer. He just poked at his food, shoulders tight.

Elton sat quietly, chewing his food, keeping his eyes on his plate.

And his brothers? They just kept their heads down, praying the spotlight wouldn't eventually shift their way.

It was an ordinary night.

Nothing special.

Nothing to remember.

But in just a few minutes, it would become a night they would never forget.

The first sign was subtle—the power flickered.

Once.

Twice.

Then a third time—before the house was swallowed by darkness.

And then—a sound.

Not a pop. Not a crackle. Not the quiet alarm of a smoke detector.

No. This was a blast.

A fire alarm of a different kind.

A pressurized canister, connected to an air horn, designed to sound only in extreme heat.

And at that moment, it was screaming.

Confusion turned to terror.

The family fumbled through the darkness, gripping the walls.

Timmy latched tightly onto his daddy's belt loop—pressed together as they stumbled down the hallway toward the living room.

As they rounded the corner, they were hit in the face with a cloud of smoke.

And then they saw it.

The ceiling was ablaze.

Flames spread across the rafters, thick black smoke curling into every corner.

The fire wasn't waiting.

It wasn't small.

It wasn't something they could put out.

It was already decided.

This house—this home—was not going to be saved.

The problem?

They lived too far from town.

There were no fire stations nearby.

No volunteer firefighters.

It's Just Me Lord, Nobody Special

No hydrants.

And the only water available—the well and pump—was frozen solid in the dead of winter.

Elton grabbed the pan of water sitting on top of the wood stove and tossed it at the fire.

But it only added fury to the ravaging flames that had engulfed the room.

The water vanished instantly.

"Get the kids out of here now before this ceiling caves in!"

Barbara rushed the boys out into the yard, completely unprotected from the bitter cold breeze.

Then she ran back in and picked up the phone.

No dial tone.

It was dead.

The fire had already claimed that too.

"It's dead!" Barbara shouted over the popping of burning timbers.

Jerry ran outside to the pump, working frantically to thaw the line.

It was hopeless.

There was nothing left to do.

Elton jumped into his truck and took off, speeding down the pea gravel road, honking his horn as he passed the neighboring houses.

Timmy could still hear him yelling, "Fire! Fire!" as he rounded the corner that led to his uncle's house, about a quarter mile down the road.

Once there, Elton made the call.

The fire department would try to come.

But they made no promises.

Back at the burning home, the family fought to salvage what little they could—throwing clothes, furniture, anything within reach, out the windows before the flames swallowed them whole.

Timmy stood in the cold, his bare feet numb against the frozen ground, watching it all.

The heat from the fire licked at his skin, yet he shivered.

Then suddenly—his heart dropped.

His new microscope was still inside.

"My microscope!" he shouted.

Without thinking, he bolted.

Timmy made a beeline through the burning house, across the hall, and into the darkness that still held control of his bedroom. Not being able to see, he had to feel his way around the room, hoping to find what he was looking for.

He could hear the crackling of the fire as it torched the rafters in the attic directly above his head.

The smoke was so thick he could taste its bitter, pungent flavor.

Then he remembered.

He lay down on the floor and reached underneath the bottom bunk—his hand landed on the plastic case that secured his most cherished Christmas present.

Target acquired.

Case in hand, he turned and ran—back across the hallway, past the crackling flames, out into the frosty night.

The house may have been lost.

But Timmy had saved his most prized possession.

But as he stepped into the cold, holding the blue case in his hands, he realized something was missing.

Jessie.

He had been standing beside him just moments before.

And then Timmy remembered—"My football helmet!" Jessie had shouted, right as Timmy took off.

He had run in after him.

Now, he was nowhere in sight.

Timmy turned back toward the house. The door still stood open, flames licking the edges, smoke pouring from the frame like breath from a monster's mouth. He froze, staring into the swirling blackness, heart pounding.

Where was Jessie?

Had he gotten turned around in the smoke?

Was he caught under something?

Had the ceiling already come down?

It's Just Me Lord, Nobody Special

Timmy's knuckles went white around the handle of the
microscope case.

He couldn't move.

He couldn't call out.

He could only watch.

It was all his fault.

He was the one who ran back into the burning house first.

Timmy's heart stopped.

But finally—a shadow in the smoke.

A figure stumbling forward.

It was Jessie.

He emerged coughing, wide-eyed, clutching something above his
head.

"I got it!" he shouted triumphantly.

In his hand—his football helmet.

But that wasn't all.

With his other hand, he raised something else.

Something fragile.

"I got the candy dish too!"

It was the glass candy dish that had sat on the TV by the front door—still half-filled with old-fashioned Christmas candy. Peppermint pinwheels, ribbon twists, little fruit-filled drops—all slightly sticky, all Jessie cared about.

Leave it to him to run into a burning house and come out with a football helmet and a bowl of hard candy.

Only then did Timmy exhale.

Then came the waiting.

There was no more water to throw.

No more furniture to save.

Only stand there and watch.

Aunt Opal saw Timmy shivering in the night air.

She picked up a rug from the ground—one that had been tossed out in the scramble to save whatever could be saved.

She didn't know it had soaked up the water Elton had thrown into the fire.

She only knew that a little boy was cold.

And so, she wrapped it around his shoulders.

Wet or not, it still blocked the wind.

It's Just Me Lord, Nobody Special

Timmy stood there in the cold, clutching his microscope, wondering what happens now.

Would this microscope mean he was going to grow up to be a famous scientist, discovering the cure for an incurable disease? Had he just secured his future?

Only time would tell.

The next morning, the family returned to the homesite, exhaustion weighing down every step.

No one spoke.

There were no words for this.

The night had been long, but there was no time to rest.

The boys had to catch the school bus.

And the parents?

They wanted to start searching through the ashes.

The sun had just begun to rise over the blackened wasteland.

Smoke still curled from the wreckage, lingering like a ghost over the ruins of what had once been their home. The air smelled of wet ashes and charred wood, a heavy scent that clung to their clothes, their skin, their hair. Even the wind carried the bitter reminder of what had been lost.

The ground was littered with half-burned memories—remnants of a life that no longer existed. A scorched photo frame, its glass cracked and clouded with soot. A melted toy, unrecognizable except for the faintest hint of color—probably Timmy's Concentration game. Fragments of furniture, now nothing more than brittle, blackened wood.

In the middle of the ruins, it still stood—the chimney. The walls were gone. The roof had collapsed. Even the floor had caved in. But the chimney stayed upright, like it had something to prove. It was new. Just built a few weeks earlier. This was its first winter. The first time the family had even used it. But corners had been cut. Something hadn't been done right. And one careless mistake had turned warmth into fire, and a house into ash. The chimney held. But it was the reason nothing else could.

Timmy climbed up onto the back of the truck, wrapping his arms around his knees as he waited for the bus. From there, he had the best view of what the fire had left behind.

It's Just Me Lord, Nobody Special

Elton had one small hope.

His coin collection.

It wasn't much—just a handful of old coins he had gathered over the years, tucked away in a tin. They had no great monetary value, but they meant something to him. A small piece of his past. Something that was his.

He searched through the charred remains, brushing aside the soot and debris, his fingers smudged black with ash. The air was still warm beneath the rubble, the heat of the fire lingering in the earth.

And then he saw it.

Not as he had left it.

Not as he had hoped.

Just a melted puddle of metal, fused together into a barely recognizable lump.

He stood there for a long moment, staring at it.

Then, without a word, he let it fall from his fingers.

Timmy sensed a bit of frustration as he continued watching from the back of the truck—Daddy kept digging, his clothes now streaked with soot, his face a mask of grime and quiet desperation. Then, from beneath a blackened pile of debris, Elton pulled something out—a long, dust-covered barrel. The wood stock was gone, completely incinerated. All that remained of his twelve-gauge shotgun was the scorched steel—faintly warm from the night before.

His daddy just stared at it.

For a moment, he said nothing. Then he raised the barrel high over his head and let loose a string of rage—raw, guttural, and unlike anything Timmy had ever heard. Words that didn't sound like his daddy. Words that cracked in the air like the fire itself.

And then—

He slammed the barrel into the ashes. Hard.

A cloud of soot and dust shot up, then drifted away in silence.

That's when Timmy saw it. The tears.

Cutting streaks down Elton's filthy cheeks.

He'd never seen Daddy cry before.

And though the moment terrified him, Timmy understood. Maybe not the words. Maybe not the fury. But he understood the loss. The kind that reaches deeper than fire and burns longer than flame.

At school, Timmy sat at his desk.

It's Just Me Lord, Nobody Special

The morning conversation had already begun.

"What did you do last night?" someone asked another.

The answers came easily.

"I watched TV."

"I played with my new Christmas presents."

One by one, each child shared their simple, ordinary evening.

Timmy stared down at his hands.

His fingernails were still rimmed with soot.

His clothes still smelled of smoke.

Someone turned to him.

"What about you? What did you do last night?"

For a moment, he said nothing.

Head bowed, fingers clenched in his lap.

Then, finally, he looked up—tears in his eyes.

And answered.

"I watched my house burn down."

The room went silent.

His teacher, seated at her desk, looked up.

Her hands paused over the papers she had been sorting.

She studied him for a long moment.

And then, without a word—"Come with me."

She led him down the hall to the school lost and found and pulled out a coat.

He hadn't even realized he didn't have one.

But she had.

She must have been watching him all morning, wondering why he had come to school without a jacket.

Now, she knew.

And though it was just a coat—just an old jacket from a lost-and-found bin—to Timmy, it felt like a warm hug from a caring teacher.

A reminder that, even after everything, kindness still existed.

The fire took everything—

Clothes. Toys. Furniture. Memories.

It left behind only ashes, smoke, and the haunting chimney…

It's Just Me Lord, Nobody Special

But sometimes, when everything familiar is stripped away, what's left is a chance to begin again.

A new place. A new school. A new start.

At least, that's what they told him.

Timmy wasn't so sure.

21 NEW SCHOOL, SAME OLD TARGET

Fire had taken everything it could from Timmy's family—
the flames swallowed up the house: the furniture, the
walls, the roof, the laughter and late-night bedtime stories.
And by the time the smoke cleared, so had Elton's decision.
It was time to leave the country behind.

For Timmy, it meant more than just moving.
It meant saying goodbye to the hills that had been his
playground, the country roads perfect for cruising on a bike or
skateboard, and the one-lane bridge where crawdads lurked
beneath the wooden planks, waiting to be caught.
And it meant leaving Big Rock—his favorite swimming hole,
where summer afternoons were spent leaping into the cool water

if he could claim a spot atop the slick surface.

The water always smelled like moss and sunlight. The jump from the top was just high enough to take your breath away before the splash. It was the kind of place where secrets were kept and dares were made. Where he felt brave, even if just for a second.

But there was one thing he didn't mind leaving behind: Gregg Mason.

Maybe, just maybe, this move would finally get the target off his back. A new school. A fresh start.

A place where no one knew him.

Where he wouldn't be the last one picked.

Central Elementary was a small school—an old school— built back when it had been the high school for the tiny community.

The steep steps leading to the entrance had been climbed by generations before him.

The gymnasium, sometimes used for the Halloween Carnival with cake walks and witches' stew, still smelled of old varnish and sweat, standing in the middle, surrounded by classrooms.

The red brick exterior still bore its name—CENTRAL SCHOOL—painted in tall, white letters beside the year 1926.

And if you looked closely, you could just make out the faded shadow of the word "HIGH" between "Central" and "School"—a ghost from its past. Ivy crept along the lower windows, and the whole place had a look that said it had seen generations come and go.

The door hinges creaked when they opened. The light buzzed overhead. Every sound echoed louder than it should have, like the building was listening.

Inside the front office, the old mimeograph machine still hummed to life, filling the air with the smell of ink and paper. Its purple-inked pages were warm and damp to the touch—handed out fresh from the machine like some kind of magic. Even years later, Timmy could close his eyes, take a deep breath, and almost smell it still.

The smell clung to his hands after he touched the paper, as if the ink itself knew it had a place in memory.

But the real test of this fresh start wasn't inside the school. It was behind it.

The playground stretched wide with monkey bars, teeter-totters, and merry-go-rounds that spun too fast, daring kids to hold on. And just beyond them—the kickball field.

It's Just Me Lord, Nobody Special

Here, the unspoken rules of childhood played out every day.

It's where your classroom ranking was put on display.

The popular kids were picked first.

Then the girls who didn't really want to play.

And then—always last—Timmy.

He felt the familiar knot in his stomach as he walked toward

the outfield.

It was happening again.

The sound of the ball hitting palms. The short, sharp commands

from the captain. The sideways glances. It was all the same

script, just a new stage.

The fresh start he imagined vanished like footprints in the dust.

It seemed... targets were transferable.

He kicked at the dry earth beneath him, watching as a dust cloud

rose and faded in the breeze.

Overhead, a flock of geese moved across the sky in a

perfect V-formation—wings beating in unison, honking as they

flew by.

Timmy tilted his head back, watching them disappear into the

distance, and wondered what it must feel like to always know

where you were going... and to not be alone when you got

there.

They didn't seem worried about being picked. They didn't have to earn a spot. They just belonged.

For a moment, he let himself wonder—as he often did: "Was there really a sign on my back that said, 'Don't pick me, I'm a loser'?"

He never could quite figure out how to escape the bullying. Across the playground, laughter rang out—loud, carefree, unreachable.

Was this really how it was going to be?

But then, he remembered something Grandma Taylor had told him.

"Timmy, God has a plan for you."

For a boy standing alone in the outfield, that was a hard thing to believe.

"For me? Really? What could He possibly plan on using me for?"

"I'm just a, nobody."

He didn't know God's plan just yet…

But maybe someday he would understand.

For now, all he could do was wait.

It's Just Me Lord, Nobody Special

Wait for things to get better.

Wait for this place to feel like home.

Wait for the day he didn't have to dread recess or lunchtime or walking into a room and scanning for an empty seat that didn't come with a sideways look.

He used to wonder if maybe it was the way he was dressed in his secondhand clothes, or the way his ears stuck out just a little. But deep down, he suspected it was something he couldn't fix— something invisible that followed him no matter where he went.

He didn't hate the new school. Not yet. But it didn't feel like it was rooting for him either.

It was like being dropped into a story halfway through. Everyone else already had their roles, their cliques, their places to stand. And Timmy? He was still trying to find the script.

And as he sat in his new classroom, staring out the window, he found himself drifting back...

Back to the hills he used to roam.

Back to the sounds of whippoorwills in the trees, the scent of honeysuckle in the air.

Back to the white house on the pea gravel road.

But no matter how many times he went back in his mind, he

could never stay long. The memories were too soft around the edges. Too far away.

He wanted to feel safe again. Wanted to believe those days weren't over. But this new world—this new school—didn't feel anything like that.

It hadn't been perfect.

But it had been his.

22 COUNTRY REFLECTIONS

Timmy sat in his new fifth-grade classroom, his elbow propped on the desk, cheek resting in his hand. Mrs. Faucet stood at the chalkboard, her voice a steady monotone, breaking down the steps of long division.

The numbers blurred on the page in front of him.

He wasn't paying attention.

His mind was somewhere else.

Somewhere warmer, where the air smelled like wild honeysuckle and fresh-tilled earth.

Somewhere that still felt like home.

Back to the white house on the road paved with tar and pea gravel.

It's Just Me Lord, Nobody Special

The house wasn't much by most people's standards—just a simple, white-framed home settled on a stretch of country road. But to Timmy, it was the world.

Everything good, everything familiar, had been tied to that place.

Like the plush green clover patches that stretched endlessly across the yard, speckled with tiny white flowers and swarming with honeybees, all buzzing lazily from blossom to blossom. He would sit cross-legged in the soft grass, with the sun warm on his neck, fingers carefully sifting through the leaves, searching for a four-leaf clover.

He never really knew what he'd do with one if he found it—probably press it between the pages of a book or tuck it into a pocket for safekeeping.

But it didn't matter.

The search itself was enough.

He liked how quiet it was when he searched. The way the bees ignored him. The way the clover tickled his ankles. It was a kind of peace—no words, no worries, just green stretching in every direction.

And when his fingers grew tired of searching, there was always something else to do.

Like weaving those tiny white blossoms into chains—long, delicate strands that became necklaces, crowns, or even Hawaiian leis, if he and Jessie were feeling extra creative.

They'd drape them around their necks, parading around the yard like kings of an imaginary island—barefoot monarchs with grass-stained toes.

Sometimes they'd try to trade the necklaces to each other like rare treasure—declaring one strand "worth two coconuts and a gold coin."

Their kingdom had no fences, just laughter, and time.

A chair scraped across the floor behind him, snapping him back just enough to realize he was still in class. Mrs. Faucet hadn't noticed. Or if she had, she didn't say anything.

His thoughts drifted again, back to the yard, back to the little rituals of country life.

Like digging for doodle bugs.

They lived in tiny cone-shaped holes scattered across the dusty ground near the porch steps and under the edge of the shed.

Timmy would crouch low, whispering, *Doodle bug, doodle bug, come out, come out,* as he gently swirled a twig in the opening.

The dirt would slowly collapse inward like a miniature landslide, and if he was lucky, out came the tiny creature—legs flailing,

jaws twitching, ready to drag the next unsuspecting ant into its

pit.

Sometimes, Timmy would drop an ant in there on purpose, just

to watch the fight.

Nature could be cruel, but to a country boy with nothing but

time and dirt, it was a real blessing.

And then there was the honeysuckle.

It grew wild along the fence line, golden blossoms hanging lazily

in the humid air.

The scent—thick, sweet, unmistakable—would drift through the

yard on a warm breeze.

Timmy had learned early on how to pull the tiny green stem

from the flower, letting a single drop of nectar fall onto his

tongue.

It wasn't much, but it was sweet.

A taste of summer.

A taste of home.

He would sometimes close his eyes while tasting it, pretending

he could bottle it up and take it with him—like a secret he didn't

want the world to ruin.

Evenings were his favorite time of day.

When the sun dipped below the trees and the sky turned shades of tangerine and lavender, the air grew cooler and the world seemed to slow down as the first fireflies blinked to life across the yard, like tiny stars.

That's when the whippoorwills began to sing.

Their lonely calls echoed from the treetops, carrying across the pasture like some old, forgotten melody.

Timmy would sit on the front porch, letting the sound wash over him, letting the night settle in.

And then—he'd yell into the darkness.

Just to hear the sound of his voice bounce back.

His echo would call to him from across the fields, repeating every syllable.

His daddy had a different explanation.

"That's the lost girl," he'd say with a twinkle in his eye.

"She's been out there for years, calling back to anyone who calls to her."

Timmy always knew it wasn't true.

But sometimes… just sometimes… *maybe he wasn't so sure.*

It's Just Me Lord, Nobody Special

He wondered if maybe she was lonely too. Maybe the echo wasn't just
sound—it was someone's way of saying, I hear you. Maybe it was God's.

His fingers absentmindedly traced the smooth edge of his
wooden school desk, but his mind was still out there—by the
creek, where the water ran clear and cool, where he and Jessie
skipped rocks, counting the number of jumps before the stone
disappeared beneath the surface.
He could almost feel the weight of a flat, smooth rock in his
palm, the way his fingers curled around it just right before he
sent it soaring.

The scent of mimosa blossoms drifted through his memory,
powdery pink petals swaying in the breeze, filling the air with
sweet perfume.
And in his mind, he was barefoot again—racing through fresh
spring grass, tasting the dust as it kicked up behind him—cool
and damp in the morning, warm and soft by afternoon.

And then—there was the green flower trick.
Find the right bush.
Grip a small branch at the base.
Strip the leaves upward in one swift motion.
A perfect little green flower remained.

The trick?

Find an unsuspecting victim.

"Hey, smell this," he'd say, holding it out like an innocent gift.

And just as they leaned in—he flicked it.

Whap, right on the nose.

Every time.

Never failed.

Classic.

Even now, the memory made the corners of his mouth tug upward, just a little.

His fingers, still caught in the memory, loosened their grip on his pencil.

It slipped from his hand and clattered to the floor, snapping him halfway back to reality—but not all the way.

His eyes stayed distant, fixed on a past that felt closer than the room he was sitting in.

"Timmy?"

The voice shattered his daydream.

His head snapped up.

Mrs. Faucet stood at the front of the classroom, one hand on her hip, the other gripping a piece of chalk.

It's Just Me Lord, Nobody Special

Every eye in the room was on him.

Heat flooded his face as he realized—she had asked him a question.

A question he hadn't heard.

A few kids snickered as he fumbled to open his textbook, but his heart was still somewhere else.

The white house on the pea gravel road was gone.

The honeysuckle, the clover patches, the creek, the long summer nights—all of it was behind him now.

But maybe... just maybe... *if he closed his eyes, he could still go home.*

But Timmy didn't have time to live in the past.

The world kept moving, and so did he.

And sometimes, the best way to settle into a new life...

Was to find the small joys waiting just around the corner.

Even if they weren't the same, even if they looked different than before—

maybe joy didn't disappear. Maybe it just trotted off into the sunset.

23 THAT AIN'T NO STICK HORSE

Timmy didn't need a rodeo. He had Princess.

She was a shaggy, stubborn Shetland pony with a mane like a haystack and a glare that said, "Don't even try it."

Her coat was the color of weathered driftwood, and she moved like royalty—when she felt like it.

Jessie's pony, Shorty, wasn't much different—short, thick-brown coat, and just as ornery.

Each summer afternoon turned into an exhilarating adventure for them.

The pasture stretched three and a half acres wide, ringed by sagging barbed-wire fences and the kind of trees that dropped sweet

It's Just Me Lord, Nobody Special

gum balls and shaded snakes.

Grasshoppers jumped ahead of every step, and dragonflies hovered

above the pond like they owned the place.

Dandelions and crawdad chimneys poked up from the ground

like little landmines, and if you weren't careful, your foot might land

in a cow patty—or worse—right in a fire ant mound.

Catching the ponies wasn't just a chore.

It was a mission.

A sweaty, breathless, sprint-across-the-pasture kind of mission.

They tried everything.

A rusted bucket of oats shaken just so.

Whistling through cracked lips.

Holding out hands like peace offerings.

But Shorty and Princess weren't fooled.

As soon as they saw the boys coming with ropes and saddles,

they'd take off—hooves pounding against the earth, tails flicking, ears

pinned back in mock rebellion.

"You get Princess, I'll head off Shorty!" Jessie would holler,

charging through the tall grass, burrs grabbing at his socks.

"I am getting her!" Timmy puffed, zigzagging behind Princess like a tired sheepdog.

The sun beat down on their backs.

Dust rose in swirling clouds.

Sweat trickled down Timmy's temples and soaked the waistband of his shorts.

The ponies danced just out of reach, darting like kids who knew the rules of the game better than the grownups.

Finally—miraculously—when they caught them, it felt like winning a war.

Timmy would loop the rope around Princess's neck, heart still thudding.

Her ears would twitch in irritation, but she didn't fight—just sighed like she was agreeing to something beneath her dignity.

Jessie would grip Shorty's rope with both hands, panting like a hound.

Then came the saddle.

Heavy leather that smelled like cracked vinyl and old dirt.

It's Just Me Lord, Nobody Special

The boys would heave it over the ponies' backs, fiddling with buckles

and cinches that never quite fit right.

The metal bit clicked against their teeth as they bridled them.

Dust puffed up from the saddle blanket.

Sometimes the ponies tried to sidestep.

Sometimes, they just stood there, bored and begrudging, waiting for

the boys to tire out.

Finally, they'd mount up—bare knees clinging to short sides,

reins in hand.

"Y'all ready for the roundup?" Jessie would ask, tipping an

imaginary cowboy hat.

"Yee-haw," Timmy answered, spurring Princess, with pretend spurs,

into a lazy trot.

They rode laps around the pasture, circling the field and weaving

between the tall trees.

Sometimes they raced.

Sometimes they played out cowboy scenes, chasing invisible bandits

or delivering pretend mail.

The air smelled like warm hay, horse sweat, and saddle leather.
The ponies' shoulders shifted beneath them, muscles moving with a
rhythm that was oddly calming.

One afternoon, after the usual half-hour chase, Timmy finally got
Princess saddled and climbed on, proud and ready to ride.
But before he could even grab the reins properly, she took off—ears
back, hooves thudding, heading straight for the trees.

Timmy ducked once, missed the second, and the third one caught
him square across the chest, sending him flying backwards off the
saddle like a sack of potatoes.
He hit the ground flat on his back—breath knocked clean out of him,
eyes wide as the sky above.
Princess didn't even look back.

Jessie doubled over laughing. "She ain't no stick horse!"
"Nope," Timmy wheezed from the ground. "She's a freight train
with a tail."

Jessie cackled even harder, nearly losing his grip on Shorty's rope.
Timmy just groaned.

It's Just Me Lord, Nobody Special

But deep down—even while picking leaves from his hair—he was still glad they'd caught her.

After ten—maybe fifteen—minutes, the excitement usually wore off.

"You wanna let 'em go?" Jessie asked, panting.

"Yeah. Let's go get some water."

And just like that, the ponies were free—ribbons of dust trailing behind them as they trotted straight to the pond to get a drink of their own.

It happened like that every time.

A thirty-minute chase for ten minutes of riding.

And still—they never gave up.

Because there was something in the pursuit.

Something in the thrill of catching what didn't want to be caught.

Years later, Timmy would think about those ponies and how much they reminded him of people: stubborn, restless, hard to pin down.

Always running when what waited for them wasn't punishment, but joy.

He figured God probably saw a lot of folks the way he saw Princess and Shorty.

Not with frustration—but with affection.

Willing to chase, to wait, to circle back again and again until we finally stopped long enough to be caught.

Some days, we run because we don't understand what's waiting.

Other days, we're just too wild-hearted to be led.

But God doesn't give up.

He just keeps coming.

And when we finally let Him take the reins… the ride really begins.

Those ponies never stayed close for long.

But the memories did—etched in dirt, sweat, and laughter; in near misses and perfect landings; in quiet afternoons when the only sound was the wind drifting through the trees.

And Timmy knew—deep down—that sometimes the best blessings are the ones you have to chase.

Especially if they come with a saddle.

It's Just Me Lord, Nobody Special

After the chase was over—after the ponies had trotted off and the saddle was hung back on the hook in the shop—the day still had room for one more adventure.

Sometimes that meant digging through the shop for a BB gun or heading down to the ditch to look for crawdads.

But the best afternoons—the ones that really hit the spot—ended with a cold bottle of Coke, a bag of salted peanuts, and a trip to the junkyard.

24 coke and peanuts

There were three things Timmy learned early in life:

Homework stinks.

Not all girls have cooties.

And—perhaps most importantly—a little pocket change could unlock a world of happiness.

At the wrecking yard where his daddy worked, sat an old Coca-Cola machine.

Its slender glass door was hiding an ice-cold bottle of Coke, just waiting to be claimed.

Drop in a coin.

Hear the soft clink.

It's Just Me Lord, Nobody Special

Pull open the door.

And there it was.

But the magic didn't stop there.

Just inside the office, above the dusty candy cabinet, sat an old metal coffee can—the owner's version of a cash register. A few more coins inside, and a boy could claim his prize: a small bag of roasted Planters peanuts.

That's when the real magic happened. Because every true Southerner knows—there's only one proper way to drink a bottle of Coke.

Pop the top.

Tear open the bag.

Dump those salty peanuts straight into the cold, fizzy drink.

The sweet.

The salty.

The crunch of softened peanuts swirling in the caramel-colored fizz—well, that was as close to heaven as a twelve-year-old boy could get.

If his daddy happened to be up front in the office, there was a good chance he'd slip Timmy the necessary funds for this sacred ritual.

A wink, a coin, maybe a playful, "Don't tell Barbara."

But most days, Elton was buried way out in the yard, lost in a sea of wrecked cars and greasy engine parts.

So, Timmy had to get creative.

That's where he and Jessie came up with a plan: aluminum cans.

Highway 67 was busy, and Arkansas had no shortage of litterbugs.

That meant two boys on bicycles—armed with trash bags and sharp eyes—could find treasure glinting in the ditches.

Skid to a stop.

Hop off the bike.

Scoop up the can.

Repeat.

Crushed beer cans. Sticky soda cans. Cans so beat-up they barely looked like cans.

If it was aluminum, it went in the sack.

Jessie had a sixth sense for spotting them.

"I got one!" he'd yell, already hopping off his bike before Timmy even saw it.

Timmy would roll his eyes. "That was on my side!"

"Finder's keepers," Jessie would grin.

They didn't care if the cans were sticky, smelly, or swarming with ants.

They were on a mission.

But collecting was only half the job.

Just a little farther down Highway 67, across from Aunt Mary Bell's house, sat a place so junky, so stinky, it made the wrecking yard look like a showroom floor: the scrap yard.

The entrance? An old gate, barely hanging on its hinges. The sidewalk? Thick metal sheets leading to a tiny front office. And just outside that door?

A rusty old scale that squealed like a dying pig when you stepped on it.

It took a lot of cans to earn enough for two boys to afford their prize.

So when their bags weren't quite full, Elton's boss would sometimes let them scavenge through the wrecked cars for more.

They'd climb through busted windows, duck under hoods, and fish around floorboards—dodging spiders, yellow jackets, and the occasional copperhead.

But every bit of grime and grit was worth it when they loaded up the scale and heard the sound they'd worked for: The unmistakable clink of coins dropping into their hands.

Victory.

Then—straight back to the wrecking yard.

For Timmy, the routine never changed.

The Coke machine.

The coffee can.

The peanuts.

A sacred ritual, never to be tampered with.

Jessie, on the other hand?

He never picked the same thing twice.

One day it was a Zero bar and a Sprite.

The next, a Payday and a Dr Pepper.

Then maybe a handful of Everlasting Gobstoppers and a few Atomic Fireballs—just to see if he could survive the burn.

His choices made no sense, but somehow, they always fit him.

It's Just Me Lord, Nobody Special

Timmy took his time.

Pop the cap.

Tilt the peanut bag just right and pour them in.

The Coke fizzed like crazy, threatening to overflow.

The smell alone—a mix of caramel soda and roasted peanuts—

made his mouth water.

Jessie's candy would be almost gone before Timmy took his

first sip.

"I think my tongue's bleeding," Jessie would say through a

mouthful of Gobstoppers.

Timmy would just shake his head and smile.

As that cold soda and softened peanuts rolled over his

tongue, Timmy knew—

No store-bought candy.

No fancy dessert.

Nothing could ever top this.

Some might have looked at those wrecking yards and seen

only junk.

But Timmy and Jessie?

They saw treasure.

Cans that turned into coins.

Coins that turned into cold drinks and candy.

And for Timmy—Coke and peanuts that turned into pure happiness.

It's funny how the smallest things—like a bottle fizzing with peanuts—could make Timmy feel like life was full of possibility.

But not every summer memory was bottled up in sweetness. Some were caught in a ditch, legs twitching in a bucket, the sound of brummp, brummp echoing in the night...

25 Frog Giggin' in Etta Bottoms

It had just rained—one of those good Arkansas showers that left everything drenched, turning dirt roads into slick paths and filling the deep ditches along the back roads of Etta Bottoms.

The night air was thick and humid, still carrying the smell of wet earth—dark and heavy—mixed with the faint, metallic tang of rain on rusted barbed wire.

Mosquitoes hovered in the muggy air, whining in their never-ending hunt for exposed skin.

And that meant one thing: it was time to go frog giggin.'

Timmy—along with Jerry, Jessie, and their cousin Tony—loaded up in the back of the pickup truck, their high-powered spotlights and giggin' poles rattling in the bed as they rumbled down the slick, dark back roads.

The tires crunched along the damp gravel, kicking up a fine mist from the puddles left behind by the recent rain.

Frog giggin' wasn't like regular hunting.

There was no sitting still. No waiting.

One person drove while the rest stood in the truck bed, gripping the side-rails tight, their spotlights slicing through the blackness, sweeping across ditches and creeks in search of the telltale glow—those tiny, glassy eyes peeking just above the surface.

And when you saw them—everything happened fast.

The brightness of the spotlight stunned the frog, freezing it in place.

Its slick green skin gleamed beneath the beam, its throat puffing and deflating like a little bellows.

Timmy stood perfectly still, heart pounding, watching someone ease their gig forward—just a foot from a fat bullfrog's head.

It was a tense moment, a mix of excitement and hesitation.

Timing mattered.

Swoosh! The gig snapped forward, slicing through the water and puncturing the frog's thick hide.

The barbs did what they were made to do—held it firm, stopped it from slipping off.

The frog kicked once, hard—its muscular legs flailing—then went limp.

One down.

Plenty more to go.

The rhythm of the night was always the same—search, freeze, gig, toss it in the bucket—over and over again.

A strange kind of music played in the background: the steady hum of the truck, the hiss of the spotlight, the croaking of frogs.

Deep, throaty brummp, brummp sounds rose from both sides of the ditch, echoing through the humid night.

But with every successful catch, those voices thinned.

On a good night, they could fill a bucket with six or seven big bullfrogs—more than enough to fry up and feed the whole crew.

Now, folks who'd never tried them always asked the same thing:

"Do frog legs taste like chicken?"

It's Just Me Lord, Nobody Special

No. No, they do not.

Frog legs taste like—well, frog.

The meat was tender, but just a little chewy.

Kind of gamey. Kind of fishy.

Like something that had lived its whole life in a muddy ditch—

because it had.

Not unpleasant, exactly.

Just... definitely not chicken.

And every now and then, those glowing eyes in the water

didn't belong to a frog at all.

Sometimes, they belonged to something longer.

Something that slithered.

Something that hissed.

A sharp breath.

A deep sigh.

Snakes.

One night, Timmy spotted a pair of glowing eyes right near

the edge of the water.

Someone aimed, gig in hand, ready to strike—when suddenly,

the "frog" moved just a little too smooth.

Not jumpy. Not hoppy. Just wrong.

They backed off quick.

Nobody was trying to spend the night in the ER with a snake bite.

By the end of it all, their hands were smeared with mud and frog slime, their shirts clung to their backs with sweat.
The metal floor of the truck bed was slick with rainwater, frog juice, and the occasional muddy boot print.
The buckets beside them were sloshing full—legs twitching in some final reflex.

They bumped along the winding back roads, the smell of wet grass and ditch water clinging to their clothes and skin.
Somewhere across the fields, a hound let out a low, echoing howl.

Tomorrow, there'd be fried frog legs on the table.

But for now? It was just a truck full of tired boys, the thrill of the night still buzzing in their veins.

Timmy didn't know it then, but nights like these wouldn't last forever.
One day, he wouldn't be standing in the back of a pickup— gripping rusted rails with muddy fingers, chasing the glow of beady eyes down a ditch bank.

It's Just Me Lord, Nobody Special

Life has a way of moving on.

And boyhood adventures have a way of turning into stories you carry with you.

But some things? They stay.

The rush of the chase.

The laughter bouncing down those country roads.

The proud weight of a bucket full of frogs at the end of the night.

And maybe—just maybe—the taste of a muddy, ditch-dwelling frog, fried golden brown, wasn't really about flavor at all.

It was about the moment.

And those?

You never forget.

Of course, not every childhood memory started in the back of a truck.

Some of the best ones had two wheels—flying down a country road, kicking up dust in the warm Arkansas sun.

And for Timmy, that kind of adventure began at Mom's.

26 ONE BIKE, TWO BIKE, TIMMY'S BIKE... GONE.

Timmy and Jerry stood just inside the house, bundled in jackets, bouncing on their heels with anticipation. Through the window, they watched the driveway—waiting for Mom's car to appear.

The scent of woodsmoke hung in the air, drifting from nearby chimneys and mixing with the sharp, crisp bite of winter. Timmy exhaled, his breath fogging the glass as he pressed his face against the picture window.

"I think I hear a car," Jerry said, shifting from foot to foot.

It's Just Me Lord, Nobody Special

Finally, Ella's car pulled up, tires crunching over gravel.
Bob was behind the wheel, and their little half-brother Craig was
beside him, playing with his hands the way toddlers do.

"Mom's here!" Timmy yelled, slamming open the screen
door.
Jerry was right behind him, both of them racing outside.

A quick kiss through the window—then the rear door flew
open.
Timmy and Jerry jumped into the back, the warmth of the car
heater washing over them.
The familiar scent of Mom's perfume filled the air—soft and
sweet, a mix of flowers and something comforting.
Something that always made Timmy feel safe.

But before heading to Prattsville, they had one more stop to
make: Poyen.

Bob pulled off the highway into a gravel driveway, where
Annette was waiting at her mother's house.
The moment the door opened, she hopped in, full of questions.

"What'd y'all get us for Christmas?"
Ella smirked. "Not telling."

"Oh, come on!" Jerry groaned.

Bob chuckled, eyes fixed on the road.

Craig, still too little to grasp the art of keeping secrets, sat quietly in the front seat, clutching his toy.

Annette, however, was determined to crack the mystery.

The next twenty miles were full of wild guesses, begging, and playful frustration.

But Ella and Bob wouldn't budge.

The gifts would remain a surprise.

Or at least… they were supposed to.

As they pulled into the driveway at Mom's house in Prattsville, the kids eagerly pressed their faces to the windows, hoping to catch a glimpse of Christmas decorations.

But Annette spotted something else.

Her eyes went wide. Before anyone could stop her, she shouted—

"BICYCLES!"

Timmy's head whipped around.

Jerry gasped.

Ella groaned. "Bobbie Eugene, you were supposed to hide

those!'"

Bob sighed, shaking his head.

There, beside the carport, sat three giant, empty bicycle boxes—completely blowing the surprise.

Someone had forgotten to stash them—and Annette had just spoiled the whole thing.

As soon as the car stopped, the kids bolted out and raced for the house.

And there, in the living room, sat the bikes.

Timmy froze—eyes locked on his.

Jerry and Annette had sleek blue 10-speed bikes, perfect for long rides.

But Timmy's?

His was different. It was perfect.

A Huffy Thunder Road—just like the ones in the Sears & Roebuck catalog—but this one was his.

The frame was sleek black with bold red and white racing stripes.

A sturdy banana seat sat high, built for speed and adventure.

But the real prize? The number plates mounted to the front and sides—"54" stamped in white—making it look like it belonged on a real motocross track.

The high-rise handlebars, wrapped in thick rubber grips—felt solid in his hands.
The knobby tires looked like they could handle anything—dirt roads, gravel, even the back pasture.
It was a bike made for a kid who wanted to go fast, jump curbs, and leave the world behind in a blur of spinning spokes.

Timmy ran his fingers along the smooth frame, a thrill running through him.

This wasn't just a bike—it was freedom.
And it was his.

That weekend, the kids rode nonstop.
The streets of Prattsville became their playground—racing, skidding, cutting corners too fast, laughing as the wind whipped past them.
They rode to Aunt Lou and Uncle Gene's house, waving at neighbors along the backroads.

Timmy's bike was everything he'd hoped for—fast, sturdy, thrilling.

But Christmas break ended. Life went back to its usual routine—weekend visits to Mom's, summer days filled with riding.

Until everything changed.

Weekend visits came to an end.

And that meant the bikes had to go home with Timmy and Jerry—to Daddy's house.

Barbara wasn't thrilled.

Jessie didn't have a new bike.

And that was a problem.

Timmy knew how things worked—if Jessie didn't have something, it somehow became Timmy's fault.

But this bike?

This was his.

And no one—Jessie, Barbara, or anyone else—was going to take it away.

He rode that bike every chance he got.

Up and down Highway 67, wind in his face, tires humming on pavement.

Past the wrecking yard.

Past the train tracks.

Freedom on two wheels.

Until one day…

It was gone.

Timmy ran outside, ready to ride.

But the bike wasn't there.

His stomach twisted.

He checked the yard. The shed. The porch.

Nothing.

Heart pounding, he stormed into the house.

"Where's my bike?"

Jessie barely looked up from the couch. "I don't know."

No smirk. No smugness.

And for once—it wasn't Jessie.

But the next day at school, Timmy got his answer.

Ricky Dean Tucker stole it.

Ricky Dean—the kid up the road.

The one who didn't ask for things.

He just took them.

It's Just Me Lord, Nobody Special

Timmy didn't hesitate.

He went straight to Daddy.

"Ricky Dean stole my bike."

Elton sighed. "How do you know?"

"Everyone at school is talking about it."

Daddy didn't like getting involved in kids' squabbles.

He believed in staying out of messes unless they found you first.

But this wasn't a squabble.

This was stealing.

That evening, Elton drove up to Ricky Dean Tucker's place.

The mobile home was run-down—patchy grass, rusted-out cars

in the yard.

Elton knocked. Moments later, Ricky Dean's grandmother

answered—arms crossed.

"My son's bike is missing," Elton said. "And Ricky Dean

has it."

Her eyes flickered. She turned and yelled inside—

"Ricky Dean Tucker! Get out here!"

A few moments later, Ricky Dean shuffled outside, avoiding

eye contact.

Elton stared him down. "Where's the bike?"

Ricky Dean hesitated. "I don't know what you're talking about."

His grandmother's eyes narrowed.

"Boy, you better not be lying to me."

Ricky Dean swallowed hard.

And then, without another word, his shoulders slumped.

A minute later, he wheeled the bike out of the shed.

Timmy's stomach dropped.

It was his bike—but it wasn't.

The sleek black frame had been smothered in cheap gray spray paint.

The number plates were gone.

Even the handlebars looked wrong.

It didn't shine.

It didn't hum.

It didn't look anything like the bike he'd gotten for Christmas.

Elton didn't say a word.

He picked it up, loaded it into the back of the truck, and shut the tailgate.

Timmy stood there, staring.

It's Just Me Lord, Nobody Special

He should've felt proud. Vindicated. Maybe even happy.
But all he felt… was hollow.

That bike didn't feel like his anymore.

It felt stolen.

It felt ruined.

It felt like something that had been taken—and couldn't be given back.

And deep down, he knew why Ricky Dean had done it.

Because he didn't have one.

Because some kids just took.

Because life wasn't fair—and didn't always try to be.

And maybe, just maybe…

That's why Timmy stopped riding it.

Or maybe…

Maybe it was something else entirely.

Something he never could've seen coming.

27 HOW THE WIND STOLE CHRISTMAS

It was December 23, 1982, just two days before Christmas. The sky had been restless all day, heavy with the kind of winter storm that didn't bring snow—but something far worse.

A violent tornado tore through a small town in rural Arkansas.

The peaceful countryside, decorated with twinkling holiday lights and festive wreaths, was suddenly plunged into chaos as nature unleashed its fury.

The wind howled like a freight train, snapping trees like matchsticks, and tossing debris through the air as if it weighed nothing at all.

It's Just Me Lord, Nobody Special

Nestled in the rolling countryside of rural Arkansas, just south of Malvern along Highway 67, stood a modest mobile home.

Surrounded by open fields and dotted with towering pines, it sat on a patch of land where the sound of cicadas filled the summer air, and the scent of wood smoke drifted from nearby chimneys in the winter.

The house had been a safe haven——a place of warmth and familiarity—where Christmas decorations hung in the windows and the glow of a porch light welcomed visitors in the night.

But in an instant, that home, Timmys home, became a toy in the storm's merciless grip.

Inside, the family was settled in for the evening.

Elton and his sons sat on the couch, playing *Asteroids* on the *Atari 2600*.

A newborn baby, Melanie, lay sleeping on the couch, undisturbed by the hum of electronic beeps and distant conversation.

Meanwhile, Barbara and Virginia stood outside on the covered patio, lingering in conversation.

Virginia, a single mother, had come to pick up her two young sons, David and DJ.

They were already buckled in the car, ready to leave.

But she had stopped to chat, unaware that the delay would endanger their lives.

Barbara's eyes caught a flicker of movement in the open field beyond the house.

She squinted, stepped closer—and there it was.

A tornado.

Twisting.

Churning.

Ripping across the land like a monster with no face.

And it was headed straight for them.

She didn't hesitate.

"Tornado!" she screamed.

The world snapped into motion.

Virginia spun around, her heart pounding.

She bolted back to the car, flung the doors open, and started yanking her boys out—one by one—arms flying, voices shouting.

"Get inside! Hurry!"

It's Just Me Lord, Nobody Special

Elton, like most men, just wanted to see it for himself.

But Barbara had no patience for sightseeing.

"No! Get down on the floor! Now!" she ordered.

And that's exactly what they did.

A moment later—the air changed.

The temperature dropped so fast, it sent a shiver through the trailer.

A deep, hollow silence.

A silence so unnatural—so heavy—it pressed against their eardrums.

And then—

The wind roared.

The walls shuddered violently.

The windows shrieked against their frames.

Before anyone had time to pray or even scream, the mobile home lifted off its foundation.

It flipped.

Once.

Twice.

Three times.

And then—it fell.

Back to the ground with a deafening crash.

For a moment—silence.

Moaning. Coughing. Crying.

Buried beneath the wreckage, Timmy's body lay lifeless.

Hands gripped his shoulders, shaking him hard.

"Timmy! Timmy! Wake up!"

The voices were urgent, desperate—but they felt far away, like echoes in a tunnel.

With a deep gasp for air, his eyes fluttered open.

But not to the world he remembered. The world around him was different.

Shadows loomed above him, jagged shapes twisting in the darkness.

The air was thick with dust, stinging his throat with every breath.

He saw it.

Or rather—he couldn't understand what he was seeing.

Everything was shattered, broken—unrecognizable.

And that's when the terror took hold.

Timmy screamed.

Not a short scream.

Not a single cry.

But a gut-wrenching, unending wail that ripped through the night.

He screamed until his lungs burned, until his throat felt raw, until hands wrapped around him, holding him still.

"You're okay! You're okay!"

The voices surrounded him, arms pulling him close, grounding him in their warmth.

But in that moment?

It didn't feel okay.

Nothing felt okay.

The world had come apart in the dark, and Timmy had woken up inside the nightmare.

The air smelled of wet earth and splintered wood.

The December cold bit at their skin, a cruel reminder that everything that had been familiar was now gone.

The mobile home no longer stood upright—it had been flipped three times and lay upside-down, just five yards from its foundation.

The Christmas tree?

Crushed beneath the wreckage.

The carefully wrapped presents were scattered, ripped open by the storm's fury.

Timmy's new stereo—the one he had been so excited about—had survived just enough to be recognized.

But its dust cover was shattered, a silent testament to how fragile everything truly was.

Neighbors rushed toward the scene, their flashlights cutting through the darkness.

The faint wail of sirens pierced the frigid air.

But the most chilling discovery came in the daylight.

The metal frame of the mobile home, the heavy structure that had once supported their walls and ceiling, should have collapsed onto them.

But it hadn't.

It was suspended—held up by Virginia's parked car and a tiny well shed, barely four feet tall.

Had either of those things not been there, the frame would have crushed them.

And if the frame had collapsed...

They would not have survived.

It's Just Me Lord, Nobody Special

Now, if you ask the ones who were there that day, they'll

tell you—there weren't just eight people in that trailer.

There were nine.

Because just like the three Hebrew children in the fiery

furnace saw a fourth man walking with them—

They believe Jesus was the ninth man in that mobile home.

The One who held the wreckage up.

The One who carried them through the storm.

The One who made sure they walked out alive.

The tornado had taken everything.

The mobile home, the furniture, the memories.

Even Christmas.

But there was no time for self-pity.

There was work to do.

28 Great Big Tornado... Itty Bitty Living Space

When the violent tornado came through, it took everything from Timmy and his family.

For the second time in just three years, they lost it all.

The mobile home.

The furniture.

The Christmas presents.

The sense of stability.

One moment, the family had a house.

The next, they had nothing.

Except for one thing. The workshop

It's Just Me Lord, Nobody Special

It wasn't much to look at—a barn-shaped structure built for fixing cars, not sheltering people.

The air was thick with the scent of grease and motor oil, a smell that clung to the walls and ceiling.

The concrete was stained black from years of spilled transmission fluid—with kitty litter scattered across the worst spots to soak up the oil.

Inside, rusted car parts lined the shelves.

Old tires leaned against the walls.

Workbenches cluttered with tools took up what little space there was.

This wasn't a place for sleeping.

It wasn't meant for living.

But walls were walls.

And a roof was a roof.

It would have to do.

Timmy looked around, taking it all in—the stained floors, the oil-slick smell, the cluttered shelves—and felt his stomach drop.

A barn? Really?

It felt like a joke.

But then, a quiet thought crept in, soft and unexpected:

"Well… if it was good enough for the baby Jesus, it's good enough for me."

And just like that, he nodded to himself.

Time to get to work.

Before they could turn the barn into a home, they had to clear it out.

Elton and the boys spent days hauling out tools, sweeping away years of grime, and scrubbing the concrete floors.

The smell of gasoline and old oil never fully went away, but after enough elbow grease, it at least felt livable.

The front of the barn had a wide opening, built for driving in cars.

Now it needed to be sealed off.

They salvaged scrap lumber from the mobile home wreckage and hammered it into place.

An old door from the trailer, still intact, was fitted into the entrance—a small reminder of the home they'd lost.

Inside, beds were lined up against the left wall near the back.

Elton and Barbara's bed sat in the far corner, separated by

nothing more than a thin comforter hung from the ceiling.

The boys' beds stretched out beside each other, one after the other, in a space that left no room for privacy.

Two donated chests of drawers sat along another wall, holding what little clothing had been salvaged.

A makeshift closet was built from a gas pipe found in the debris, supported by scrap wood.

Clothes hung from the bar, but everything smelled faintly of smoke and motor oil.

At the front of the barn, just inside the door, sat a real electric cookstove.

They could at least cook meals properly.

But with very little space, everything had to be crammed on the old workbenches.

The refrigerator, due to electrical limitations, had to sit on the opposite side of the barn near the closet—a daily inconvenience, but one they worked around.

The living room was carved out of what had once been the back-right corner of the shop.

A wood stove—an ancient relic from days gone by—sat near the wall, heavy cast iron with a stovepipe that carried smoke up through the tin roof.

The cold, hard concrete floor made the space even harsher.

That's when they remembered the carpet remnants. Scattered in the debris of the destroyed mobile home were pieces of carpet—not full sections, just scraps and leftovers. Some were torn.

Others were frayed.

But they were better than bare concrete.

Piece by piece, they patched together a floor. The colors and textures didn't match, but no one cared. For the first time since the storm, something felt soft underfoot.

It wasn't much.

But it made the barn feel a little less like a workshop—and a little more like home.

They even had a phone—a rotary one, mounted to the wall in the corner.

Elton had put it in years earlier, and it came in handy. If he needed something from the house—or if supper was ready—someone just picked up and called.

It's Just Me Lord, Nobody Special

Now, it was where Barbara would spend most of her evenings talking to her mother.

The Arkansas winter showed no mercy.
The old wood stove worked overtime, glowing red-hot.
But the barn had no insulation, and the wind found every crack.
No matter how much wood they burned, the warmth never fully reached the far end of the barn.

Some mornings, ice crystals formed on the inside walls.
The boys could see their breath before even stepping outside.

Blankets were piled high.
And the fight for who got to sleep closest to the stove was real.

There was no running water.
The well had survived, but there was no plumbing to the shop.
Water had to be carried in.
That task fell to Timmy.

Day after day, he hauled water in a big orange cooler—pumping it full, lugging it inside.
Over and over.

When people asked if they had running water, Elton would grin and say:

"Oh, we've got running water—Timmy runs to the well, fills a bucket, and runs it back."

The bathroom situation wasn't much better.

Barbara's daddy built them an outhouse from salvaged lumber, piecing it together with whatever he could find.

The only real luxury was a toilet seat—rescued from the wreckage.

The nights were long.

But stormy nights were the worst.

The tin roof amplified every raindrop, turning even a drizzle into a deafening roar.

When the wind picked up, it whistled through the cracks in the planks, chilling the air no matter how hot the stove burned.

And when lightning split the sky, the memories of that December tornado came rushing back—along with the fear that it could happen again, that another storm might come roaring through and rip their world apart

Those nights, the boys lay in bed, counting the seconds between the flash and the thunder, remembering the night they lost everything.

And yet... the barn held.

It's Just Me Lord, Nobody Special

For over a year, the barn was their home while the new
house was built.

It wasn't just Elton working day and night.
Several men in the family were skilled carpenters.
The effort was led by Elton's brother-in-law, Benny.

Lumber was measured and cut.
Bricks were laid.
The house began to take shape—slowly but surely.

And then, on May 5, 1984—Timmy's sixteenth birthday—
the family finally moved in.

It was beautiful. A three-bedroom brick house with a big
bay window in the back, two bathrooms, and a floating bar
between the kitchen and living room.

After a year in a barn, this wasn't just a house.
It was a palace.

The barn?
It still stands today.
A silent witness to a family that refused to be beaten by a storm.
A reminder that even when life takes everything—faith,
determination, and love can rebuild it all.

They made it through the storm.

Through the cold.

Through the crowding.

Through the barn.

By the time they moved into the new house, it felt like they'd finally earned a breather.

Timmy was ready to get back to a normal routine—back to everyday school life.

But nothing ever stayed normal for long.

There was always something waiting to shake things up.

And it came.

Just months later.

A paintbrush.

A bad decision.

And one thing he didn't know—this was gonna be a Thriller.

29 THIS IS GONNA BE A THRILLER!

Back when he graduated from sixth grade at Central Elementary, Timmy had one thought on his mind: starting over.

New school.

New building.

New chances to not be...

well, Timmy.

Malvern Junior High wasn't just a small step up—it was a whole different world.

Grades seven through nine, all crammed into a maze of brick hallways, buzzing bells, and sweaty lockers.

It smelled like pencil shavings, cafeteria food, and teenage body spray.

You had to change classes between periods, memorize a locker combination, and learn how to survive as a small fish in a very big pond.

Timmy was fourteen and still trying to figure out if anyone would ever take him seriously.

It was also the year of the tornado.

And the year Timmy failed another grade—not because he wasn't smart, but because trauma doesn't show up on report cards.

But in the middle of all the chaos, there was one class that gave Timmy a reason to get out of bed in the morning: art.

And the man behind it? Mr. Welcher.

Mr. Welcher wasn't like the other teachers.

He didn't bark orders.

He didn't glare down from behind a desk.

He moved through the room like it was a workshop, not a classroom.

His jeans were speckled with dried paint and clay, like they hadn't seen a washing machine in years.

His shirts usually had at least one mysterious smudge of charcoal or glaze.

Art class was held in a portable building, separate from the main school, tucked away like a hidden studio.

You had to walk a long sidewalk to get there, and when it rained, that sidewalk turned to a slick, muddy trail.

But once you stepped inside, you knew it was special.

This wasn't kindergarten arts and crafts.

This was the real deal.

Just inside the door on the right sat a full-size kiln, used to fire clay projects once they'd dried.

Along the wall—beneath a row of windows—ran a long cabinet with a sink, stained with a rainbow of years' worth of rinsed brushes and washed hands.

One wall displayed papier-mâché sculptures in various stages of completion—some from advanced classes, others still dripping wet with paste.

Color wheels lined another wall, each hand-painted by students.

Mr. Welcher made them mix every shade by hand—just to prove there were more than eight colors in a Crayola box.

It's Just Me Lord, Nobody Special

Shelves were stacked with boxes of clay, plaster molds, brushes sorted by size, and jars of well-used paint with cracked lids.

The room smelled like creativity—paint, glue, and warm dust.

Timmy loved it there.

It was the one place he didn't feel like an outsider.

In art class, it didn't matter if you were cool, popular, or even particularly talented.

You just had to try.

And Timmy tried.

But even your favorite place isn't always safe when you're Timmy.

One morning, he walked into class expecting to pick up where he'd left off on his papier-mâché sculpture.

But instead of the usual setup, Mr. Welcher was knee-deep in pep rally prep.

The school's pep squad was putting on a big performance of Michael Jackson's Thriller, and the task had officially fallen on Mr. Welcher to help build the props.

That meant giant cardboard tombstones, leaning against the walls in various stages of ghostly gray.

He was painting them with a big two-inch-wide brush—the kind you'd use on a fence, not a fine art piece.

Timmy walked in and, naturally, couldn't resist.

"You missed a spot," he said, pointing at one of the tombstones.

Mr. Welcher didn't look up.

"That one's leanin' like the Tower of Pisa... you paintin' graves or landmarks?"

Still no reaction.

Just tighter brush strokes.

Timmy smirked.

"You sure you know what you're doing with a brush that big?"

Mr. Welcher finally stopped mid-stroke and looked over, straight-faced.

"I'm warning you," he said.

"If you don't go on and leave me alone, I'm gonna whap you with this paint brush."

Timmy grinned.

"No, you won't."

WHAP.

The brush hit him square across the face.

Cold, thick gray paint smeared from cheek to cheek, dripping down his nose like wet cement.

He just stood there, blinking—like someone had unplugged his brain.

The class gasped.

A few kids laughed.

Timmy? He was frozen.

And then came the final blow.

There was a perfectly good sink just a few feet away—water running, paper towels nearby.

But Mr. Welcher, maybe still steaming from too much prep and too little patience, just pointed to the door.

"Go clean up… in the main building."

So Timmy—face streaked in paint—walked.

Across campus.

In front of everyone.

Some laughed.

Some stared.

Nobody asked.

And Timmy?

He walked with his head down, thinking:

Of course this would happen to me… because I'm Timmy.

He didn't mean to cause trouble.

Not really.

Sometimes, it just found him—like gray paint on his face, or

laughter trailing behind him as he crossed campus alone.

But sometimes, the trouble wasn't in the paint.

It was in the noise.

The lights.

The twisting, flipping, looping feeling of losing control—

And a little voice inside whispering, "You've been here before."

30 Past Tornado, Stupid Decision

Magic Springs was a small amusement park tucked away in the foothills of Arkansas, just outside of Hot Springs.

It wasn't massive.

It wasn't flashy.

But to a kid from the country—to Timmy—it really was magic.

The parking lot was paved with asphalt, radiating heat like an open skillet.

The bus doors creaked open, and the wave of humidity hit like a wall.

Timmy stepped out and immediately felt the soles of his shoes soften against the burning pavement.

It's Just Me Lord, Nobody Special

He could already smell the park from here—fried food, sunscreen, and the mechanical oil of nearby rides.

He flashed his ticket at the entrance, and an attendant stamped the back of Timmy's hand with invisible ink.
It looked like nothing—until you held it under the blacklight just past the gate.
Then it lit up like a secret code, proof that you belonged.

Inside, the park was alive.

The sound of kids screaming from high above on the swings, the distant clack-clack-clack of a roller coaster climbing its first hill, and the steady beat of music pumping through tinny speakers all blended into a summer symphony.
The log flume ride sprayed bursts of water into the air.
The Sky Hook loomed tall in the distance, lifting guests high into the sky, where they could look down on the entire park—and beyond it, into downtown Hot Springs.

A long, covered bridge extended across the pond, with fish food for sale in gumball machines, allowing you to feed the hundreds of hungry catfish just below the surface.

Food carts were scattered throughout the park—selling hot dogs, frozen chocolate-dipped bananas on a stick, and lemonade so sugary it left your teeth buzzing—taking every opportunity to draw money from hungry guests.

Carnival-style games offered inflatable hammers, unicorns, and penguins as prizes, hung high on sun-bleached racks that smelled like rubber and dust.

But none of that held Timmy's attention.

He was staring at The Roaring Tornado.

It wasn't a massive roller coaster by today's standards.

But to a kid, it looked like a steel monster.

You climbed a long, tall staircase to the top, stepped into the car, got strapped in, the coaster dropped down a steep hill, flipped upside down once, then climbed back up the other side—and then did the whole thing again, backward.

That was it.

Two loops.

No corkscrews.

No tunnels.

Just two upside-down moments.

One going forward.

One coming back.

It's Just Me Lord, Nobody Special

Timmy had stood at the base of that coaster more times than he could count.

Each time, he'd tell himself this would be it—this would be the day.

But when he looked up at that steel loop, his knees locked. His chest tightened.

His stomach turned.

He'd made it through the turnstile at the bottom, only to duck back under.

He'd climbed halfway up the stairs, then turned around— dodging oncoming thrill-seekers like a salmon swimming upstream.

More than once, he made it all the way to the top, stepped into the car... and then right back out the other side, heart pounding, throat dry, avoiding eye contact the whole way.

It wasn't just nerves.

It was dread.

He wasn't afraid of roller coasters.

He loved them—especially the big wooden one that didn't go upside down.

But this?

This was different.

For most kids, a roller coaster was a thrill.

For Timmy, it was a trigger.

It was PTSD.

After surviving a real tornado in seventh grade—one that tore through his world and left everything upside down—The Roaring Tornado roller coaster felt personal.

Too personal.

It wasn't just a ride.

It was a loop that brought everything back.

The screaming.

The spinning.

The helplessness.

He wasn't just scared of going upside down.

He was scared of feeling like that again.

And even worse—he was scared of being watched.

Judged.

Laughed at.

Timmy had been the butt of jokes before.

Quiet kid.

It's Just Me Lord, Nobody Special

Weird kid.

The one who always sat alone at lunch.

The one nobody picked unless they had to.

He'd learned how to fade into the background.

But now, with classmates around him and no escape, he felt anything but invisible.

This trip? This was a class trip with the junior high choir, and the pressure was on.

Everyone had lined up to ride.

A few kids had teased him when he hesitated earlier in the day.

This time, he had no excuse.

No way to hide.

His pride marched him up every step of that towering staircase.

But inside, his heart wasn't just pounding—it was pleading.

Don't make me do this.

His legs felt like Jell-O.

His hands were clammy.

His breath came in short bursts.

Half of him wanted to bolt.

The other half knew—this was the moment.

And somehow… he stayed.

He sat down.

He pulled the seatbelt across his lap and clicked it shut.

He yanked the shoulder bar down and made sure it locked.

Then he closed his eyes, gritted his teeth, and held on.

The car lunged forward.

Toward the first drop.

Clack.

Clack.

Clack.

And then—FWOOOOSH.

Down the drop, wind tearing past his face.

Into the loop.

Upside down.

And up the hill on the other side.

And just like that, it was over—almost.

It still had to go back.

Timmy barely had time to process it before the ride started

rolling again—this time in reverse.

He braced himself as the car dropped backward into that same

loop.

It's Just Me Lord, Nobody Special

Two seconds of disorienting, stomach-flipping chaos.

Then the car climbed the hill and rolled to a stop.

It was over.

He was alive!

He opened his eyes.

He had done it.

He climbed out of the car and stepped onto the exit platform with shaky legs and sweaty palms.

Timmy smiled.

It wasn't a big moment to anyone else.

But to him, it was everything.

One loop.

One moment of courage.

One memory that would outlast the cotton candy and the thrill of the ride itself.

And in that moment, Timmy realized something he hadn't fully understood before:

Fear doesn't disqualify you from faith.

You can be scared and still move forward.

You can be shaking and still be strong.

God never said we had to feel brave—only that we had to trust Him enough to try.

That day, Timmy didn't just face a roller coaster.

He faced his past.

His fear.

His silence.

His shame.

And with one click of the seatbelt and a shaky exhale, he decided—I'm not sitting this one out anymore.

Because sometimes, bravery isn't loud.

It doesn't come with applause or fanfare.

Sometimes, it just looks like a quiet kid on a hot summer day, finally daring to stay in his seat.

Timmy had faced his fear—twice.

Not just sitting, but staying, even when everything in him wanted to run.

But in small towns, the past doesn't always stay in the past.

Sometimes, it finds a way to loop back around.

And for Timmy, the past had a name.

Ricky Dean Tucker.

31 WELL, THAT BACKFIRED!

By the time Timmy had been in junior high a couple of years, he figured he was finally done with Ricky Dean Tucker.

They'd both gone to Central Elementary once upon a time, but that felt like a different life—back when recess was king, and the biggest threat was a pop quiz or a spilled lunch tray.

Now they were deep into junior high—different routines, harder classes, and new faces.

It should've been a fresh start.

But one thing hadn't changed: Ricky Dean still knew how to ruin a good day.

And Timmy had been having one of his best.

It's Just Me Lord, Nobody Special

He was still riding the high from the weekend before—
when he, Jerry, and Jessie had piled into Jerry's candy apple red
'65 Ford pickup and driven up to Little Rock for a live wrestling
event at Barton Coliseum.
Packed wall-to-wall with screaming fans, the air inside smelled
like a mix of popcorn, hot dogs, and locker-room odor.
The lights overhead were blinding, and the bodies in the ring
moved like comic book characters come to life.
Timmy had never seen anything like it.

And at the merch table, he found it—a light blue sleeveless
Rock & Roll Express shirt, with Ricky Morton and Robert
Gibson mid-fight in bold print across the front.
Timmy had bought it with his own money—earned by selling
buttons he made with his Badge-a-Minit button machine.

It felt like more than just a shirt—it was a reward, a memory
stitched in cotton.
It was his.

When Monday morning rolled around, he didn't even mind
heading to school.
He slipped the shirt on with care, brushed off a stray thread, and
slung his bag over his shoulder.

He rode the school bus, bouncing down the gravel roads of rural Arkansas, the windows cracked, the smell of vinyl and diesel thick in the air.

He didn't expect compliments.

He didn't expect anyone to care.

But for once, Timmy felt proud.

A little bigger.

A little louder on the inside.

The day dragged by—as all days do when going from class to class—and by seventh period, English class, he was counting down the minutes until the bell rang.

The sun streamed in through the windows that overlooked the courtyard, and Timmy could see the car riders already making their way to the pickup lanes.

The chalkboard behind the teacher's desk was streaked with the ghosts of that morning's grammar lesson, faded verbs and sentence fragments still clinging to the slate.

Timmy sat near the front, doodling in the margins of his notebook.

The room buzzed with quiet chatter, desks squeaking, pencils tapping, shoes scuffing against the floor.

It's Just Me Lord, Nobody Special

Behind him sat Ricky Dean Tucker.

Timmy didn't trust him.

He hadn't since the bike incident.

Ricky Dean had a mean streak a mile wide and a look on his face

like he was always on the edge of doing something dumb.

He hadn't said anything all class.

Just sat there.

Too quiet.

Then the teacher stepped into the hallway to stand at her

door and monitor the halls for when the bell finally rung.

And in the span of five seconds—everything changed.

Timmy felt a burst of heat between his shoulder blades.

Sharp and hot, like someone had pressed a match to his skin.

He flinched forward in his seat, twisting around in time to see

Ricky Dean snap a silver cigarette lighter closed and slide it into

his pocket.

Timmy's hand went to his back.

The fabric was warm.

But he didn't know how bad it really was.

Not yet.

The bell rang soon after, and everyone grabbed their books and spilled into the hallway.

Timmy rode the bus home, the shirt clinging to his skin in the late-afternoon heat, the faint smell of something scorched following him all the way.

It wasn't until he got home and peeled the shirt off that he saw it.

A perfect hole.

Burned through the fabric.

The edges black and stiff.

The faint scent of burned cotton still lingered.

He stood there in his bedroom, holding it up.

This wasn't some old shirt from a box of hand-me-downs.

This wasn't something Barbara made him wear because it still had life left in it.

This was his.

His money.

His pick.

His memory.

"Timmy!" Barbara's voice echoed from the bedroom door. "What happened to your shirt?"

Elton stepped in, took one look at the damage, then turned to his son.

"You need to take that shirt to school tomorrow," he said, calm but firm.

"Take it straight to the principal's office."

So, he did.

The next morning, Timmy folded the shirt and tucked it carefully into his backpack.

Mr. Chenault didn't laugh.

He didn't ask what Timmy had done to provoke it.

He looked at the shirt and said, "I'll take care of this. Go on to class."

Then he called Ricky Dean Tucker to the office.

Ricky Dean came in slouching; hands jammed into his pockets.

"Did you burn this shirt?" the principal asked.

Ricky Dean didn't deny it.

Just shrugged.

"You're gonna pay for it."

"I ain't got money," he mumbled.

"I live with my grandma."

"Then you'll pay for it a little bit at a time until it's paid for," the principal said.

And that's exactly what happened.

Each week, for several weeks, the principal called him to his office and handed Timmy a small envelope—usually with a dollar, maybe two, crumpled bills with a little bit of sweat still on them.

Once, there were coins rattling in the corner.

It was awkward at first.

Getting called out of class.

Walking down the hall alone.

Opening that envelope in silence.

But week by week, it began to feel like something more.

Not justice, exactly.

Not revenge.

Just—acknowledgment.

That shirt had meant something.

And for once, someone said—this matters.

But still, for weeks after, Timmy found himself checking over his shoulder in the hallway.

Even when Ricky Dean kept his distance.

It's Just Me Lord, Nobody Special

Even when the envelopes came like clockwork.

The fear didn't disappear just because someone said it mattered.

But it helped.

It helped to know that grown-ups noticed.

That damage could be seen.

And that, maybe for the first time, someone stood up—for him.

He kept the burned shirt for a long time.

Folded and tucked away in a drawer—like a relic.

Not as a reminder of Ricky Dean's cruelty, but of what it cost to finally be seen.

And what it meant when someone said:

This wasn't your fault.

By the time the smoke settled—both literal and emotional—Timmy wasn't the same kid.

The burn had healed, but the scar ran deeper than skin.

That shirt, that moment, that principal's office... it all left a mark.

Not just a lesson about bullies, but about standing up, being seen, and realizing that sometimes, you have to fight for what's yours.

Timmy didn't say much more about the shirt.

There wasn't much to say.

Some things you don't fix—you just feel.

But even a day that starts in ashes can end with headlights on a

gravel road, a movie screen in the distance, and the hope that—

just for a little while—you might lose yourself in the glow.

32 Growing Up Under the Stars

Timmy grew up under the stars.

Not the kind you wished on—but the ones that flickered across a giant outdoor movie screen while engines idled and popcorn spilled onto the floorboard.

The Malvern Drive-In had been part of his life for as long as he could remember.

Some of his earliest memories weren't at school or even at home—they were at the drive-in.

Friday evenings felt different.

The sun would still be hanging low, and you could feel the air start to shift.

Barbara would announce it: "We're going to the drive-in," and the house would erupt.

Jessie and Jerry would race off to change clothes, yelling about who called shotgun.

Timmy tried to sneak into the front seat first—but he was usually blocked.

Barbara stayed in the kitchen, popping popcorn by the potful and dumping each batch into a clean trash bag lined with paper towels.

They weren't about to pay those outrageous concession prices.

While the popcorn cooled, the boys loaded the car with lawn chairs and a blanket—just in case they were allowed to sit outside.

Someone always forgot something: a flashlight, mosquito repellent, an extra bag of chips.

Timmy would get sent back inside, only to return and find the best seat already taken.

Daddy would pat the roof and say, "Let's move out," and off they'd go, gravel crunching under the tires.

On the ride over, the windows were cracked just enough to let in the smell of fresh-cut grass.

Jessie and Jerry elbowed each other for seat space while Barbara laid down the law: "You better behave, or we're going straight home."

She never meant it—but she said it every single time.

Cars lined up early, headlights off, waiting for the gates to open.

You turned right at the entrance, where an attendant counted the heads in your car and took your money.

Then you'd swing wide around the back of the screen and ease into your spot.

Each space was marked by a metal pole with a silver speaker box hanging on a hook.

You'd roll your window halfway down, clip the speaker to the glass, and there you were—ready for the show.

Back then, Daddy would pull into a spot halfway back. Timmy and his brothers couldn't see much from the backseat, so if they really wanted to watch, Daddy let them climb onto the hood—on one condition: don't block the view.

That was the deal.

But if the movie was boring?

That's when the real fun started.

It's Just Me Lord, Nobody Special

The boys made a beeline for the playground just beneath
the screen.

Tall monkey bars stood proudly under the glow of the projector,
and kids would swing, slide, and climb while movie scenes
played overhead.

Cars idled here and there, headlights blinking off one by
one.

Somewhere in the distance, a rowdy group of people could be
heard—just loud enough to blend with the sound of frogs.

Neighbors waved across windshields.

A few families laid out quilts like picnic blankets while others
reclined in open truck beds with pillows and coolers.

The merry-go-round was the biggest attraction—and for
good reason.

It was small, but fast.

If you could find someone willing to push, you could lie flat on
your back and spin so fast it felt like flying.

Jessie always pushed the hardest.

Timmy once rolled off, dizzy and grass-stained, giggling but
always ready to jump back on.

There was even a speaker nearby, though Timmy never could figure out who was supposed to be watching the movie with their neck cranked toward the sky.

But it didn't matter.

That playground was the place to be—especially during intermission.

They didn't visit the concession stand.

Not once.

Barbara was tight with money and wasn't about to pay those prices.

Instead, she'd pass the trash bag full of popcorn from the front seat like it was a sacred offering.

Tucked under the seat were boxes of candy—Milk Duds, Twizzlers, and Whoppers.

Some stuck to their wrappers; others rattled inside the box.

In the trunk, an ice chest sloshed with melting ice and a variety of ice-cold cokes—most in aluminum cans with sharp little pull tabs you had to be careful not to step on.

Timmy was always fascinated by the beam of light shooting out of that tiny window in the projection booth.

How could something so small fill a whole screen?

But sure enough, by the time it reached the front, it stretched wide across the night—dust and bugs dancing in the glow, the film flickering and popping—like magic.

One night, just before the movie started, a bat flew right through the beam, casting a giant flapping shadow across the crowd.

Jessie ducked like it was a missile.

Timmy laughed so hard he nearly dropped his speaker box.

He remembered another night even more vividly.

Not because it was funny—but because it stayed with him.

Where the Red Fern Grows.

Now, looking back, he remembered climbing up on the hood of the car, knees pulled to his chest, the speaker hissing softly beside him.

It wasn't just a movie—it was a moment that stayed with him forever.

He looked around, half-expecting to see someone else crying too.

Maybe even Old Dan or Little Ann trotting across the gravel lot, straight off the screen.

That's how real it felt.

Like the movie wasn't just playing—it was reaching down, touching something tender in his chest he didn't know was there.

But the real magic wasn't just the movies.

It was the sound of frogs in the distance, the faint laughter drifting over from another car, the itchy blanket across the hood, and the way Daddy would mumble something funny during the boring parts—just loud enough to make the boys giggle.

It wasn't just family time.

It was freedom, wonder, and togetherness—wrapped up in a gravel lot, under a summer sky.

Timmy didn't know then that those nights would become memories.

That the speakers would go silent.

That the playground would rust.

That the beam would flicker for the last time.

He just knew he was there.

And it was magic.

And maybe that's what made it so special.

It's Just Me Lord, Nobody Special

For a boy who rarely felt seen—who was used to being the
one in the back seat, the one sent back inside, the one squeezed
out of shotgun—those nights gave him something steady.

A place where the world slowed down.

Where nobody had to be important to feel important.

Not at the drive-in.

Not under those stars.

It wasn't grand.

It wasn't loud.

But it was his.

And somehow, that was enough.

Timmy grew up under the stars.

And for a little while, it felt like the stars smiled back.

Those nights at the drive-in gave Timmy wonder.

But the steady hands that anchored his world?

Those belonged to Daddy.

33 Farther Along

You could set your watch by it.

Saturday mornings, right about the time the dew burned off the grass, you'd find Timmy's daddy, Elton, stretched out beneath a car.

Just a simple alligator jack, keeping a ton of steel suspended above him.

His legs stuck out, radio blaring country music, and a grease-stained rag tucked in his back pocket.

The sun would just be starting to climb above the trees, casting long shadows across the driveway. A fresh layer of dust settled over the hood of the car, soft and golden in the early light. The air smelled faintly of gasoline and cut grass. Birds chirped lazily in the trees above, occasionally startled into flight by the clang of metal or the bark of a neighbor's dog.

If you got close enough, you might hear Elton holler, "Hey! Who is that? C'mere!" he'd yell—he couldn't see from where he was lying, but he could always hear one of the boys running around the yard.

Then, with a nod toward the front of the car, he'd say, "Hand me that ranch."

Now, anyone unfamiliar with Elton's southern twang might've started looking for a bottle of Hidden Valley.

But Timmy knew better.

His daddy just needed the grease-covered 5/16 Craftsman wrench that had slipped out of reach.

It might be half-hidden in the grass or balanced on the edge of the fender, catching the sunlight just right. But Timmy always found it.

Elton was a mechanic by trade, but it wasn't just a job—it was who he was.

Monday through Friday, he worked at the wrecking yard.

His uniform never changed: dark blue Dickies pants, and a light blue, short-sleeved button-up shirt.

On the right, a patch with the company's name.

On the left, a patch that simply read Elton—stitched in red thread.

A small but fitting reminder of who he was: a working man, a provider, someone who got the job done.

No matter how hard Elton scrubbed, the grease never truly left his hands.

His knuckles were usually busted—evidence of a stubborn bolt or a wrench that slipped.

And by the end of every day, there was always a dark smear on his cheek where he'd wiped away sweat with an already-dirty hand.

His fingernails stayed stained in that dark gray half-moon, a permanent mark from years of turning wrenches. His elbows were calloused. His boots, always the same old pair, left dusty prints across the carport.

But for Elton, the work didn't stop at five o'clock—not when there was always a side job waiting on the weekend.

A neighbor's truck that wouldn't crank.

A carburetor that needed adjusting.

It's Just Me Lord, Nobody Special

A problem for most folks—but not for Timmy's daddy.

He knew every part of a car like the back of his hand.

Timmy had grown up watching him work.

He'd sit nearby on an overturned bucket, kicking the dirt,

mesmerized by the way Daddy's hands moved—steady, sure,

never rushed.

Sometimes he'd ask questions—"What's that part for?" or "Why

won't it start?"—and Daddy would explain it as he worked,

using words Timmy half-understood, pointing with his wrench,

drawing invisible diagrams in the air.

It didn't matter if a bolt was rusted in place or if the engine

wouldn't turn over.

Daddy never lost his cool.

He didn't raise his voice.

He didn't throw tools across the yard like some men did.

Even when something slipped and busted a knuckle wide open,

he'd just shake it off, wrap it in the rag, and keep going. His calm

was part of what made him feel strong—like nothing could

knock him off balance.

No, when things got tough, he'd lean back, wipe his hands on

that rag, and jump right back in.

It was a simple life, yes—but one full of trials.

Losing not one, but two homes to natural disasters would be enough to bring most men to their knees.

But not Elton.

His resilience kept him going.

And if you were lucky enough to pass by while he was working, you might hear him whistling.

Timmy heard it all the time.

And the tune? Always the same one.

After everything he'd been through—trying to feed a family of five, recovering from disaster after disaster—Elton's favorite song never changed:

Farther along we'll know all about it,

Farther along we'll understand why.

Cheer up, my brother, live in the sunshine,

We'll understand it all by and by.

Sometimes he'd hum it under his breath while pulling off a valve cover. Other times, he'd whistle it full and clear, like he wasn't just passing the time—but declaring something true.

Now Elton is in his eighties.

The mind that once remembered every nut and bolt, every

shortcut and trick of the trade, is fading.

Dementia has taken a lot.

But I'd be willing to bet...

Somewhere, in the quiet of his mind...

He's still whistling *Farther Along*.

Timmy never realized it then, but looking back now, he can see it plain as day—his daddy had a way of making things work, even when the odds were stacked against him.

Maybe that's where Timmy got it from.

He didn't have all the tools.

He didn't always know what he was doing.

But like Elton, he kept going.

Kept trying.

Kept showing up.

There were days when the road felt long, when hope ran thin, when everything inside him whispered to give up. But he didn't. Because he'd seen what it looked like to endure. He'd seen it in grease-stained hands and busted knuckles and a man who never once let hardship take his joy.

And sometimes, just like his daddy taught him—when you roll up your sleeves and lean into the moment—you find something worth holding onto.

Not in a toolbox.

Not under the hood of a car.

But in the most unexpected places.

34 THE MONKEY MADE ME DO IT

Timmy never quite knew why his parents divorced.

That wasn't something grown-ups explained to little boys in those days—especially boys who were too young to understand the weight of the words, yet old enough to feel the ache that came afterward.

What he did know... was that every other Friday, his heart would race with excitement because it meant one thing—time with Mom.

Ella had remarried, and with her new husband came a new family—a stepsister named Annette, a half-brother named Craig, and a house that, for two short days at a time, felt like home. Those weekends felt like borrowed magic—short, sweet bursts of time when the ordinary turned extraordinary, and the scent of Mom's shampoo lingered every time she hugged him tight.

A bike ride to the ice cream shop.

A drive-up Petit Jean Mountain.

Maybe—just maybe—a trip to Hot Springs, Arkansas, where tiny, glistening crystals lay buried beneath the dirt…

But no adventure could outrun Sunday afternoon—the part that never got easier.

The fun faded into silence.

Timmy and his brother packed their bags with heavy hands, dreading the slow drive back, where the seat felt colder and the air quieter.

And just like that, the magic was over.

Then one day, the goodbyes became even harder.

Ella sat them down and broke the news—she was moving.

Not just across town.

Not just a few hours away.

No, she was leaving Arkansas altogether.

She was moving… to Texas.

When Ella said the word Texas, it didn't register at first.

Timmy pictured cowboy hats and tumbleweeds—things he'd

only seen on TV.

But the part that stuck was this: it was far.

Too far for weekends.

Too far for a quick visit.

It felt less like she was moving states…

and more like she was moving to another planet.

Timmy cried.

For days, he cried.

He didn't know when he'd see her again.

Would it be months?

Years?

To a child, time is a mystery.

And for Timmy, the mystery was unbearable.

But summer came.

And with it, a promise kept.

For the first time ever, Timmy was going to Texas.

Ella and Bob were helping on a ranch in North Texas—
wide open land as far as the eye could see, filled with cattle,
rolling hills, and adventure.

While he was there, they took him to Six Flags.

It's Just Me Lord, Nobody Special

But even bigger than that—at least to Timmy—was the biggest flea market he had ever seen, Canton, Texas.

Now, if you've never been to Canton, let me tell you—it was like stepping into another world.

The air was thick with the scent of kettle corn and leather, and every turn brought a new surprise: rusted signs, toy soldiers, old records, handmade quilts, and tables piled high with memories for sale.

Timmy wasn't looking for anything in particular that day. He was just along for the ride.

But what he found... would change his life forever.

There, among the endless tables and booths, sat a puppet. A monkey.

Not just any monkey, but one with long arms and long legs, designed to wrap around your neck as if it were clinging to you for dear life.

Something about it caught Timmy's eye.

He reached into his pocket, handed over his money, and walked away with his very first puppet.

He named him... Josh.

He practiced in front of mirrors, in front of the babysitting kids, anywhere he could find an audience.

At first, it was just silly stuff—hello, goodbye, silly voices.

But then the monkey started to talk back.

Not really, of course, but in Timmy's hands, Josh came alive.

And for the first time, Timmy didn't feel so alone.

He had no idea… that in those simple moments of play, something far bigger was happening.

A seed had been planted.

A fire had been lit.

Because that monkey?

That scruffy little puppet from a Texas flea market?

That monkey was just the beginning—of something Timmy couldn't even imagine.

And though Josh would only be part of his life temporarily, Timmy never forgot where it all started.

Josh was a small discovery that led to something bigger.

But when summer ended, and home came calling… life went on as it always had.

It's Just Me Lord, Nobody Special

And one summer afternoon, standing on a makeshift baseball field, Timmy found himself in a different kind of moment.

One that had nothing to do with puppets...
And everything to do with pain.

35 THE BALLPLAYER

It was a scorcher of a summer afternoon in Malvern, Arkansas—the kind of day where the heat rippled in waves over the pastures, cicadas screamed from the trees, and the scent of sunbaked earth and fresh cow patties hung heavy in the air.

Timmy and his brothers found themselves right in the middle of it all, playing baseball the only way they knew how—with whatever they could find.

Jessie had just joined Little League, and he was eager to practice his out fielding.
Determined, he grabbed his brand-new Spalding baseball glove and took off toward the far end of the makeshift field—right into the middle of a cow patty minefield.

It's Just Me Lord, Nobody Special

"Good luck out there!" Jerry called, smirking as he twirled the bat over his shoulder.

Jessie wrinkled his nose, carefully stepping over a particularly fresh pile.

"This better be worth it."

Jerry grinned.

"It is—for me."

He patted the bat against his palm.

"I guess that means I bat first!"

Timmy frowned.

He wasn't thrilled about that.

"Fine! But I get to bat next!"

"Sure, sure," Jerry said with a shrug.

"But pitch to me first."

Timmy looked around their makeshift field, taking in the patchy grass and uneven dirt.

Home plate? A piece of plywood that had once been part of an old sign.

First base? A hubcap from the wrecking yard.

Second base? A milk jug filled with just enough dirt to keep it from blowing away.

Third base? A flat rock that had cracked someone's toe more than once.

And the pitcher's mound?

Not a real mound, mind you—no groomed dirt or chalked lines. This was just the rusted cover of an old 1965 Ford pickup's air intake, half-buried in the grass.

But in Timmy's mind?

It was Yankee Stadium.

He wasn't just some barefoot kid in the Arkansas heat.

He was Nolan Ryan.

And thousands of fans were watching.

He gripped the ball, adjusting his stance, narrowing his eyes at his opponent—his older brother, Jerry, who stood at home plate, tapped his bat against the plywood like he was in the World Series.

Timmy took a deep breath, went into his wind-up …
and fired the ball ten feet over Jerry's head.

Jerry ducked, then shot Timmy a glare.

"Come on, man! Throw me something I can hit!"

Timmy huffed, wiping the sweat from his forehead.

"Fine."

He shuffled a few steps closer, adjusted his grip, and tried again.

This time, the ball floated in slow and steady—a perfect pitch.

Jerry swung.

CRACK!

The bat connected beautifully, sending the ball soaring straight back at the mound.

Straight at Timmy's face.

For a split second, time froze.

Timmy's eyes went wide as he saw the ball spinning toward him, the red stitching blurring together.

His brain screamed: Move!

His legs, however?

They didn't get the message.

The ball made impact with a sickening thwack!

Timmy's head snapped back, his vision exploding into white light.

Then came the pain.

It radiated through his skull, throbbing like a jackhammer behind his eyes.

He let out a groan and crumpled to the ground like a sack of potatoes.

Jessie and Jerry rushed to his side.

"You okay?"

Timmy groaned.

"No. I'm dead."

Blood poured from his nose, his face already swelling like a balloon.

He wasn't sure what had hit him—Jerry's bat or a freight train.

They hauled him inside, half-dragging, half-carrying him, where Barbara was already waiting.

She took one look at him, let out a sigh, and did what any good Southerner would do.

She flung open the freezer and grabbed the first thing she could find.

Not an ice pack.

Not even a cold rag.

She pressed a bag of black-eyed peas against his face, holding it firmly in place.

Timmy yelped.

"Ow! That's cold!"

Barbara didn't budge.

"Good."

And as Timmy lay there, face throbbing, he had to admit…

If there was ever a literal reason to use black-eyed peas…

This was it.

For the next week, Timmy's reflection told the whole story.

Two black eyes. A swollen nose.

And the unmistakable look of a prizefighter on the losing end of

a heavyweight bout.

His dreams of becoming the next Nolan Ryan?

Over.

He wouldn't have known how to say it then—but maybe

getting knocked down was part of the plan.

Grandma Taylor would've said so.

Not that he believed it yet.

But one day… maybe he would.

Timmy had taken some hard hits before.

But this one?

This one hurt.

A baseball to the face had been bad.

But what really stung … was what came next.

Because the next time he found himself face-to-face with a battle—it wasn't on a ball field.

But it was in the cow pasture after a heavy rain.

36 crawdad battles

It was a well-known fact among country boys that the best time to go crawdad hunting was right after a good rain. That's when the ground stayed soft, the puddles hadn't dried yet, and the little creatures were busy fortifying their underground fortresses.

The air was thick with the smell of wet grass and fresh earth.

In the pond, a giant bass broke the surface, leapt into the air, and splashed back down—sending a ring of ripples across the water as steam lifted where the sun was beginning to break through.

Timmy knew what to look for—small towers of rolled-up mud balls, scattered like tiny castles across the back field.

It's Just Me Lord, Nobody Special

Each one marked the entrance to a crawdad's hidden lair.

Jessie called them "mud chimneys."

Timmy just called them targets.

"Over here!" Jessie hollered, spotting one of the tallest

chimneys he'd ever seen.

Timmy grinned as he scanned the ground.

A few yards away, another one stood like a monument to its

builder.

"I found one over here!" he called back.

And just like that, the battle had begun.

Down went the chimneys, smashed beneath eager hands.

Then came the real work—digging.

They both dropped to their knees beside the mud towers,

elbows deep in the earth, feeling blindly through the dark,

twisting tunnels.

"Gotta feel the fight," Timmy said.

The trick was to go slow... very slow.

Because if you weren't careful—

Snap!

"Aaagh!" Jessie yelped, jerking his arm out of the hole. Dangling from his finger was an angry crawdad, clamped down like a steel trap.

Timmy doubled over laughing.

"Looks like he found you first!"

Once they wrestled Jessie loose, they examined their catches.

Jessie's was massive, its thick pincers raised, ready to fight.

Timmy's was battle-worn, a scrapper who had likely seen his share of wars.

Now came the moment of truth:

A battered '65 Ford hubcap as the battleground.

Two fearless warriors—pincers raised—ready for combat.

And a crowd of two mud-covered boys, breathless with anticipation.

Jessie cupped his hands to his mouth.

"Ladies and gentlemen, in this corner—Hackclaw Jim Digger!"

Timmy chimed in.

"And in this corner, The Underdigger!"

It's Just Me Lord, Nobody Special

They set the crawdads down.

For a long moment, nothing.

Just two mud-streaked gladiators, sizing each other up.

Then—Timmy's crawdad made the first move, lunging forward with a snap of its pincers.

Jessie's fighter recoiled, then struck back.

The two locked claws, twisting, turning, legs kicking up dust in a furious battle for dominance.

"Oh, it's a close one!" Jessie hollered.

"Look at that grip! Look at that footwork!"

"Do crawdads have feet?" Timmy asked.

"They do now!"

And then—just like that—it was over.

Timmy's crawdad stood victorious, pincers high like a tiny, muddy prizefighter.

Jessie scooped up his fallen warrior.

"You'll live to fight another day, Clamps."

They lay back in the wet grass, arms behind their heads, the hubcap between them like a little arena that had seen its final fight.

Jessie lobbed a stick into the air and let it fall back to earth.

"We good? Or should I start the rematch?" he asked.

Timmy didn't answer right away.

"Nah," he finally said.

"Let's let them go."

He could hear the ponies in the distance—Shorty whinnying, Princess snorting at something in the brush.

The crawdad in his hand gave one last twitch before Timmy knelt and let it go—back into the same mud it came from.

Jessie wandered toward the gate, dragging his stick behind him.

The sun was beginning its slow dip behind the trees.

And just like that, the battle was over.

All that effort.

All that digging.

The risk, the pain, the chase—just to find the best.

The toughest.

The strongest.

And yet, in the end, no matter how mighty those crawdads seemed...

they were still just small, fragile creatures, buried in the mud until someone reached down and pulled them out.

It's Just Me Lord, Nobody Special

And isn't that just like us?

We fight, we struggle, we battle to prove ourselves.

We try to be the strongest, the smartest, the toughest.

But the truth is, we're all stuck in the mud—trapped in our own sin—until Someone reaches down and pulls us out.

And that's exactly what Jesus did.

He didn't leave us in the dirt.

He came down, reached into the mess, and lifted us out.

Not because we were strong enough…

But because He loved us enough.

Timmy sees it now—those battles weren't pointless.

They were a glimpse of a much bigger one.

Because the greatest champion of all… had already fought—and won—for us.

Some victories came with glory.

Others?

They came with barbecue sauce.

And if there was one thing Timmy and Jessie knew for certain…

A bag full of Q-Burgers was worth any mission.

37 THE Q-BURGER MISSION

It was the 1980s in a small Arkansas town—a time when two boys on bicycles could roam freely, their only concern being how far their legs could carry them.

And on this particular summer day, Timmy and Jessie had one thing on their minds.

Not adventure.

Not mischief.

No, sir.

Food.

It's Just Me Lord, Nobody Special

Not just any food—a Q-Burger.

Now, for those unfamiliar, a Q-Burger was no grand sandwich.

It wasn't stacked high with toppings or slathered in fancy

condiments.

No.

It was a humble thing.

A soft bun.

A modest portion of shredded barbecue.

Just enough sauce to make it stick.

And yet… for two hungry boys with a couple of crumpled

dollars in their pockets, it was nothing short of a treasure.

Because at just 25 cents each, a boy could feast like a king for the

price of a handful of aluminum cans.

But there was just one problem.

Popplo's Pizza—home of the legendary Q-Burger—was not just

around the corner.

Not close at all.

It was five miles away—on the opposite side of Malvern.

And five miles in the summer heat, on banana-seated bikes

without gears, was no small feat.

But when you're thirteen, armed with bicycles and a craving that just won't quit—five miles is nothing.

They set off, pedaling past the wrecking yard, where the sound of clanking tools and the hum of an air compressor faded behind them.

The wrecking yard had its own unique scent—a mix of grease, rust, and old motor oil baking under the summer sun.

The smell clung to the air, to their clothes, even to their skin some days.

But today, the scent was replaced by something even stronger...

Hunger.

And maybe something else too—at least for Timmy.

The farther he pedaled, the lighter he felt.

It wasn't just about food.

It was about space.

About getting away for a while.

There were days when the walls back home felt a little too close.

Where the air felt thick, where his stepmom was constantly barking orders, causing way too much tension.

It's Just Me Lord, Nobody Special

But out here—riding with Jessie and the wind in his face—he could finally breathe.

There was something sacred about riding with a purpose. Not just to eat—but to go.
To be gone for a little while.
To put some distance between themselves and the noise of home life.

Ahead, Highway 67 stretched long and straight, the heat rippling in waves off the pavement.
It was the kind of heat that made the air shimmer, distorting the world ahead like a desert mirage.

Cars whizzed by, kicking up bursts of hot wind that smelled like asphalt and cut grass.
The boys pedaled on; their shadows stretched long across the pavement.

No helmets.
No cell phones.
No backup plan.
Just an open road and an empty stomach.

They pushed harder, sweat dripping down their backs, their legs burning as they climbed each hill.

Every downhill stretch was a blessing—a chance to coast, to let the wind cool their faces before the next incline forced them back into a battle against gravity.

They passed houses with porches stacked high with firewood, yards with barking dogs that lunged at chain-link fences, a few kids playing barefoot in driveways, their laughter carried away by the wind.

And then—before they even saw the sign... they smelled it. That unmistakable, mouthwatering tang of barbecue.

The scent curled through the air—thick and smoky—making their stomachs tighten with anticipation.

It was the kind of smell that stuck to your clothes, that seeped into your memory, that made your mouth water before you even realized it.

Their legs ached, their shirts clung to their backs, but as they pulled into the parking lot, they grinned.

They had made it.

They dropped their bikes in the gravel out front and walked up to the window, sun still hot on their backs.

The woman inside leaned out beneath the little awning, a notepad in her hand, waiting.

It's Just Me Lord, Nobody Special

Timmy dug into his pocket and pulled out a sweaty dollar and a few coins.

Jessie did the same.

They each ordered four Q-Burgers.

No fries.

No drinks.

Just pure, messy, delicious goodness.

A few minutes later, their order came through the sliding window in a grease-stained paper sack.

They took it to the picnic table nearby—weathered wood, paint peeling, the kind that rocked a little if you leaned too hard on one side.

And that's where they feasted.

Timmy took the first bite—and for a moment, the world paused.

He could taste the sauce, smoky and sweet.

The meat, warm and tender.

The soft bun, a little squished from the tightness of the paper wrapper, but perfect all the same.

He leaned back, wiping his mouth with the back of his hand, and let out a satisfied sigh.

Freedom tasted like sauce on a soft bun.

He looked across the table at Jessie, who was already halfway through his second burger.

They didn't say much.

They didn't need to.

Sometimes the best conversations happen in silence, between two brothers who know the same hunger—of the belly and of the heart.

And when the last crumb was gone, and their fingers were sticky with barbecue sauce, they hopped back on their bikes.

The sun hung lower in the sky now, stretching golden streaks across the horizon.

But something else had changed—

the clouds.

What had been a bright, cloudless afternoon was now shifting.

The sky had darkened in the distance, thick gray clouds rolling in, swallowing the sun at the edges.

It's Just Me Lord, Nobody Special

Timmy nudged Jessie.

"We better hurry."

Jessie looked up, squinting at the sky.

"Think we can beat it?"

Timmy grinned.

"Only one way to find out."

And with that, they took off.

The ride home wasn't like the ride there.

It was a race against the storm.

Their full stomachs begged them to slow down, to let their

bodies rest—but there was no time.

The air had changed—cooler now, the kind of cool that meant

rain was coming.

Their legs burned.

Their tires kicked up dust.

Every crack of thunder in the distance made them pedal faster.

They reached the wrecking yard just as the first raindrop

splattered onto the pavement.

By the time they skidded to a stop in the driveway,

breathing hard, hearts pounding, the sky had opened up.

The rain poured down in sheets, soaking the road they had just traveled.

Jessie let out a breathless laugh.

"We made it."

Timmy wiped the sweat from his forehead, watching the storm roll in.

"Yeah."

And they had.

Because that's what summer was.

Not just hot days and free time.

But work, rewards, and the kind of freedom only a kid on a bike could know.

However, Q-Burgers weren't the only reward worth working for.

Some things took more than a few aluminum cans to earn.

And for Timmy, that meant long days in the summer sun—

Elbows deep in vines.

Hands-stained purple.

And the sound of a cannon booming across the field.

38 THE THINGS WE DO FOR A DOLLAR

I t was an Arkansas summer, sometime in the early 1980s. The air was thick, the sun was unrelenting, and in the quiet fields just off Highway 67, the work had already begun. Because if a boy wanted money back then, he didn't ask for it— he earned it.

Across the road from Grandpa Taylor's house was a farm, owned by a man named Hypo Porter.

Every year, Mr. Porter planted acres upon acres of purple hull peas, growing enough to sell by the bushel at the Malvern farmer's market.

But peas don't pick themselves, and Mr. Porter, being just one man, couldn't do it alone.

It's Just Me Lord, Nobody Special

So, he made an offer.

Three dollars per bushel.

Now, three dollars might not sound like much today, but back then—when minimum wage was $3.35 an hour—it was gold to a thirteen-year-old boy.

For Timmy, the work started early—before the sun had fully risen, before the heat could melt a man where he stood.

Sometimes, Barbara, wanting to make a few extra dollars, would go pick peas as well.

She'd come into Timmy's bedroom before the sun was even waking up, tap him on the head, and say:

"Timmy, get up! We need to go before it gets hot."

That was the signal.

Timmy would scurry out of bed, throw on his pea-picking clothes, and they'd head to the fields.

The morning dew still clung to the leaves, soaking his shoes, turning the dirt into thick, sticky mud.

The vines, heavy with pods, left deep purple stains on his hands as he plucked them one by one, dropping them into the growing pile in the basket.

They each grabbed a smaller basket to harvest in and set the bigger bushel basket at the end of their row, so they didn't have to lug it around.

Once they chose their row, the picking began.

It wasn't a race against each other, but it was a race against time.

They wanted to get as many bushels as possible before the sun got too high in the morning sky.

It wasn't glamorous work.

It wasn't easy work.

But it was work that paid.

And then—just when Timmy had found his rhythm—came the explosion.

No, it wasn't a war zone.

That was just Mr. Porter's cannon.

The peas weren't just popular with folks at the market. They were a favorite among deer, crows, and every other critter looking for a free meal.

So Mr. Porter built a contraption that let out a thunderous boom every thirty minutes, shaking the ground and echoing across the hills—a warning to all scavengers:

These peas are not for you.

The first time Timmy heard it, it nearly knocked him off
balance.

After that? It was just part of the job.

Pick. Boom. Fill. Weigh.

Pick. Boom. Fill. Weigh.

By mid-morning, the baskets were full, their muscles ached,
and the sun had begun its slow takeover of the sky.

That was the signal.

It was time to weigh in.

Mr. Porter was a busy man.

He didn't have time to stand around watching his hired hands
pick peas—there was always more work to do.

But he made sure things ran smoothly.

He had two fields stretching as far as the eye could see—
one just behind his house, about a half mile up on a hill, and the
other right next to Grandpa Taylor's house.

When Timmy and the others had filled their baskets, they
didn't have to go hunting for Mr. Porter—he was always at
home, ready for weigh-in.

Under his carport sat the scale, along with stacks of empty bushel baskets waiting to be filled.

And there he'd be, standing in his usual attire—faded overalls, a light-colored button-up, and that straw hat, worn just right like it had been shaped to his head over years of hard work.

Mr. Porter wasn't the kind of man to bark orders or demand perfection.

He had a quiet way about him, a patience that set him apart from some of the other men in town.

He appreciated hard work, but more than that, he respected the ones who showed up and did their best.

And maybe that's why he was Timmy's favorite bus driver.

Every morning during the school year, that same man who weighed their bushels would be waiting behind the big steering wheel of the yellow school bus.

Unlike some drivers—who always seemed to have a permanent scowl—Mr. Porter greeted the kids with kindness.

He wasn't just the man running the pea fields.

He was the man who made sure they got to school safe.

Who never made them feel small.

Who had a tender heart hidden beneath that hardworking exterior.

And for a kid who spent his summers racing to beat the heat and fill just one more basket, that kind of kindness mattered.

When Timmy's basket hit that scale, he held his breath. No shortcuts. No half-baskets. Thirty-three pounds, or it didn't count.

Now, sometimes Barbara wasn't picking to sell—she was picking to can for the family.
And when that was the case?

She had a little trick up her sleeve.

She'd pick the peas, pack them down, pick more, pack them down—sometimes even have Timmy stand on them (gently, of course) to sneak in a few extra pounds.

But Mr. Porter wasn't a dummy.
He would weigh every bushel and bring it right back down to thirty-three pounds.

It was worth a shot—but there was no getting past him.

And when that scale tipped just right, when Mr. Porter nodded in approval and reached into his pocket, there was no better feeling in the world.

Three dollars per bushel.

Hard-earned money in a boy's hand.

And money in his pocket meant he had options.

The bowling alley? Tempting.

Arcade games, a jukebox, and pool tables waiting to swallow up every quarter he had.

The skating rink? Always a possibility.

The dream—finding a girl to couple skate with.

The reality—skating backward, all alone...

Because let's be honest, nobody was lining up to hold hands with Timmy.

Timmy wasn't just working for money.

He was working for something to look forward to—something he could call his own.

Every dollar he earned in those pea fields—every blister, every mosquito bite, every thundering boom of that cannon—was a step toward that something.

He didn't know it yet, but all that sweaty work was leading somewhere unexpected.

Not to a farm. Not to a field.

But to an idea—crazy, bold, and for an easy fifty bucks, weird enough that a young boy might just dare to be stupid.

39 Dare To Be Stupid

Timmy wasn't the kind of kid who went looking for the spotlight, but one day, the spotlight found him—right there in the middle of Walmart during Brickfest, Malvern's annual celebration of being the Brick Capital of the World. As part of the festivities, the store decided to hold a lip sync contest.

Nothing fancy.

Just a local event with a few prizes and some buzz.

To most people, it might not have meant much.

But to Timmy, the fifty-dollar first-place prize was everything.

It represented a stack of cassette tapes.

Maybe a new shirt.

Maybe even something brand new that hadn't been worn by somebody else first.

It wasn't just money—it was dignity.

It was hope.

It was freedom.

He couldn't do it alone, so he started talking to his friends at school.

Frank was the first to say yes, and Daniel didn't take long to follow.

They weren't performers by any means, but they liked Weird Al—and that was enough to form a plan.

The idea? 'Girls Just Wanna Have Lunch.'

A parody of a pop hit, loud and ridiculous in all the best ways.

Timmy would take the lead while Frank and Daniel sang backup.

None of them had ever done choreography before, but that didn't matter.

They had heart.

And they had guts.

They practiced night after night in the carport at Timmy's house.

Concrete underfoot.

Crickets chirping in the trees.

Sweat dripping down their necks as they flailed and stomped and tried to keep a beat.

Timmy stood in the middle, mouthing the lyrics with wild eyes and swinging elbows while Frank and Daniel flanked him with exaggerated motions and off-beat swaying.

The smell of cut grass and summer heat hung heavy in the air.

Every time they ran the routine, Timmy grew more confident.

A little louder.

A little goofier.

A little weirder.

And for once, he didn't care what he looked like doing it.

So, he did something wild.

He went downtown and rented a camcorder.

It was the kind you had to carry with both hands—big and clunky, with a thick strap and a lens cap that swung like a yo-yo every time it moved.

Timmy had to leave a deposit and promise not to break it.

He didn't care.

It's Just Me Lord, Nobody Special

He just knew this performance had to be captured.

It wasn't just fun—it was history.

He asked Frank's sister to run the camera.

She agreed—probably thinking they were insane but amused

enough to play along.

And that was enough.

Show day arrived.

Timmy woke up buzzing.

He feathered his hair with a part down the middle and locked it

in place with half a can of Aqua Net.

Then he slipped on his silky black button-down shirt, made sure

Frank and Daniel had on their white ones, and they piled into his

green Ford Granada—hearts pounding like jackhammers.

Calling it a stage was generous.

It was just a cleared section of tile in the children's clothing

department, near a crooked plastic table with a cassette player

and a microphone that didn't even work.

Shoppers wheeled carts full of school clothes.

A toddler screamed in the toy aisle.

The overhead speakers buzzed with something between static

and elevator music.

But Timmy didn't care.

This was it.

Time to be stupid.

They were third to perform—right after a girl who lip-synced to 'Manic Monday' by the Bangles.

Frank's sister hit RECORD, and Timmy stepped into the glow of the ceiling lights.

And he went for it.

He mouthed every silly lyric with full-body commitment—arms flailing, face contorted in mock hunger, eyes darting like a cartoon character gone rogue.

Frank and Daniel chomped and staggered behind him like confused backup dancers.

It was unpolished.

It was loud.

It was hysterical.

Some shoppers paused to watch.

A few laughed.

A baby cried.

Somewhere in the distance, an employee paged a cleanup crew

to aisle twelve.

Timmy didn't even notice.

For two minutes and fifty-one seconds, he was center stage—leading the weirdest show Malvern had ever seen. And then... it was over.

The crowd—if you could call it that—scattered.

The tape kept rolling for an awkward beat before she hit STOP.

The judges sat behind a folding table—a makeshift judging stand—scribbling notes.

One of them was Barbara's sister—Timmy's step-aunt.

He'd noticed her from the beginning.

Figured she'd be fair.

A few minutes later, the winners were announced.

Timmy and his crew? Second place.

No trophy.

No confetti.

No envelope with fifty bucks.

Just a short ovation and a pat on the back.

Timmy didn't say anything.

But deep down, he knew.

They'd won that contest.

They just hadn't been allowed to win it.

Still—second place wasn't nothing.

Not for a kid who spent most of his life in the background.

That moment—ridiculous, sweaty, and entirely too public—had mattered.

Because little moments stack up.

A kid in a black shirt, mouthing Weird Al in front of a clearance rack, finally daring to be seen.

Finally daring to be silly.

Finally daring to believe.

Timmy didn't know it yet, but every silly moment, every laugh, every wild idea—all of it was building something.

A voice.

A sense of self.

A belief that maybe, just maybe, he was becoming somebody.

He didn't know what that meant yet.

He didn't have a plan.

But something had shifted.

For the first time, Timmy wasn't just reacting to life—he was reaching for it.

It's Just Me Lord, Nobody Special

That performance, that moment of joy and boldness, was more than just a memory.

It was proof that he could be seen.

Maybe even remembered.

But boldness doesn't always guarantee belonging.

Because being "somebody" comes with risks.

And the world has a way of reminding you where you stand.

Soon enough, Timmy would leave behind the safety of silliness...

and step into a place where the lights were harsher, the rules stricter, and the crowd?

Not always kind.

Because the next spotlight he stood under wouldn't come with a laugh track.

It would come with pressure.

With a paycheck.

With people who didn't care where he came from—only how fast he could move.

And it all began the night the drive-in went dark.

40 Fade to Black

Just up Highway 67 South, between the new brick house and the wrecking yard where Elton worked, stood one of Timmy's favorite landmarks: the Malvern Drive-In.

It was a place where memories were made.

Timmy didn't just grow up going there—he grew up working there.

At fifteen, Timmy found himself employed at the very place he had spent so many childhood weekends.

The Malvern Drive-In became his first job.

It wasn't just familiar; it felt like home.

Before long, he was running the concession stand—flipping burgers and sliding drinks across the counter like a pro.

He knew which machine was temperamental, how to dip a corndog in hot oil without burning it, and how many boxes of popcorn it took to survive a Saturday night double feature.

He liked the rhythm of it: the way dusk fell, and headlights blinked on one by one.

The hush that came with the opening credits.

He made minimum wage—$3.35 an hour—which didn't sound like much at the time, but to him, it was gold.

Most nights, he worked about four hours in the concession stand, where the air was thick with the smell of butter and grease.

His job? Popping endless tubs of popcorn, pouring ice-cold Cokes, flipping sizzling hamburgers, and crisping up golden fries for hungry moviegoers.

It wasn't glamorous—but it was honest work.

And best of all—it was his money.

Real money.

And that meant freedom.

There was just one problem.

Timmy didn't have a car.

Not yet.

Every night when it was time to go to work, he hopped on his 10-speed bicycle and rode down the highway to the drive-in. Getting there was fine—it was still daylight, and he could see the road.

But getting home? That was a different story.

The highway had no streetlights—just a wall of blackness pressing in on either side.

Pedaling home in complete darkness wasn't just difficult—it was downright terrifying.

The only sound was the hum of his tires and the occasional rustle in the roadside weeds, which made his heart beat a little faster.

So, when Timmy received his first paycheck, he knew exactly what to buy: a bicycle headlight kit.

He went straight to Walmart and bought a set that included a front headlight, a rear taillight, and a tiny generator.

The generator attached to the bike's frame and rubbed against the back tire, creating power for the light as the wheel turned. The faster he pedaled, the brighter it shone.

Most nights, he rode home at a normal pace, just happy to see where he was going.

But then there were the weekends, when the drive-in hosted a double-feature horror marathon, Timmy pedaled home a whole lot faster.

Something about Freddy Krueger or Jason Voorhees looming on the big screen made the dark highway feel a little too eerie.

More than once, he must've looked like a human light bulb streaking down the road—his headlight flaring brighter with every desperate push of the pedals.

The job didn't make him rich, but it gave him something even better—independence.

For the first time, Timmy was buying his own clothes. No more hand-me-downs or off-brand leftovers.

He picked out shirts that matched his style, shoes he actually wanted, and even splurged on something bold—leather pants.

Yes, leather pants.

It was the '80s—don't judge.

After saving up a little more, he made his biggest purchase yet: a brand-new trampoline.

His siblings loved it, and even the kids Barbara babysat got to enjoy it—bouncing for hours in the front yard, their laughter rising with each springy jump, arms flailing, hair flying in every direction.

But it wasn't just about the money.
It was about having something of his own.

Timmy had learned a lot at the drive-in—how to work, how to earn, and how to stand on his own.

But then, everything changed.

It was the last night of the season—just another Sunday on the schedule.
Sundays were usually slower.
Most families were already home, getting ready for the week ahead.
The crowd was light.
The concession line never really formed.
Everything felt a little quieter than usual.

And that's when his boss showed up.

It's Just Me Lord, Nobody Special

Glenda managed both the drive-in and the Ritz Theatre
downtown.

When she pulled up that night, Timmy knew something was

different.

She didn't usually come around on Sundays.

She called Timmy and his coworker aside and told them

what they didn't expect to hear.

"This is it," she said.

"We won't be opening next season."

Timmy blinked.

"Wait, what?"

Glenda nodded.

"After tonight, it all gets boxed up.

It's being moved downtown."

Just like that, it was over.

The popcorn boxes.

The drink cups.

The movie reels.

All of it was going to the Ritz.

Timmy didn't know what to say.

He'd spent so many nights there—working, watching,

remembering.

It wasn't just a job.

It was a part of who he was.

But Glenda wasn't done.

"I can offer you a position at the Ritz," she said.

"You can start there next week."

The Ritz.

Downtown.

Indoors.

Open seven days a week.

Matinees on Saturday.

And Friday nights? That's when the crowd showed up.

Not movie lovers.

Not families.

Just teenagers looking for a place to hang out.

Timmy had heard the stories—rude customers, loud talkers, kids

who tossed popcorn and gummy bears at the screen.

Some even stuck the gummies in their mouths first so they'd

really stick.

It wasn't going to be burgers and corndogs anymore.

The Ritz had popcorn, candy, drinks, and hot dogs.

It's Just Me Lord, Nobody Special

That was it.

Smaller menu.

Bigger nerves.

He accepted the job.

He needed it.

He couldn't remember what movies played that final night at the drive-in.

But he remembered the feeling.

Like something was ending.

And something else was beginning.

It wasn't loud.

It wasn't dramatic.

Just a quiet close to a chapter he didn't want to end.

But maybe—just maybe—that's how growing up works.

You don't always get a finale.

Sometimes, the reel just runs out.

And the lights come up.

And the stars overhead?

They're still shining.

Even when the screen goes dark.

And maybe that's where faith comes in—trusting that when one story ends, God is already preparing the next one.

Even if you can't see the screen yet.

THING 2 ENTER STAGE RIGHT

The Ritz Theatre sat in the heart of downtown Malvern, tucked between the shops like it had always been there—because it had. Once a grand, single-screen cinema with velvet ropes and balcony seating, it had been converted into a three-theater multiplex. One screen downstairs, another beside it, and the old balcony—once reserved for segregation—had now been transformed into a third screen with stairs leading up behind the concession stand.

Friday night arrived, and with it, a line of restless teenagers stretching down the block. The sidewalk buzzed with noise— kids laughing, shoving each other, gripping wrinkled dollar bills in sweaty fists. The line began at the box office and wrapped around the corner, disappearing into the dark. Timmy stood behind the concession stand, peeking out at the growing crowd.

Inside, the popcorn machine was already running. Glenda's rule was simple: when the first customer walked through the door, the popcorn had to be popping—bursting out of the kettle, filling the air with buttery temptation. She said it lured them in—and if they didn't want a drink, that's what the extra salt was for.

This machine was newer than the one at the drive-in. There was no need for scoops of oil—just a button that measured everything perfectly. Next to it, the hot dog warmer spun slowly, keeping a dozen all-beef wieners rotating in hypnotic rhythm. The candy rack was fully stocked with overpriced Haribo gummy bears and those spicy cinnamon Hot Tamales everyone seemed to love. Timmy was ready—or at least, he hoped he was.

Andy stood beside him—cool and collected. He'd been at the Ritz for a while and knew the ropes. He was already training for the projection booth but still helped at the concession stand during rush hour. That night, he was training Timmy. Andy handled the customers, and Timmy filled cups, passed out popcorn, and tried not to get in the way.

Glenda stood near the front doors—arms crossed, eyes sharp. She monitored the flow of people like a traffic cop,

318

making sure the line kept moving and no one underage tried to sneak into the R-rated movie.

The moment the doors opened; the lobby turned into chaos. Popcorn flew. Candy wrappers rustled. Teenagers shouted. And through it all, Timmy worked the counter, sweating under the pressure but holding his own.

When the last kid rushed off to their seat and the movies started rolling, there was a moment to breathe. But the lobby looked like a war zone: popcorn strewn everywhere, cups half-smashed on the floor, napkins balled up and tossed in corners. Timmy and Andy pulled out the brooms and sweepers and got to work.

But the breaks never lasted long.

Every Friday night, it seemed, there were complaints. Unruly kids. Loud groups. Someone tossing candy or yelling at the screen. And when that happened, Glenda acted fast. First, she sent Andy into the theater with a flashlight to give a warning. Second strike, they got a personal escort to the office. Third strike? Out on the sidewalk with a warning not to come back next week.

After a few weeks, it was Timmy's turn.

Andy handed him the flashlight. "Your turn," he said with a smirk. And just like that, Timmy became part of the Friday night enforcement crew. He stepped into the theater, scanned the seats, and called out the noisemakers. It was awkward at first. But over time, he found his voice.

He gave warnings.

He escorted troublemakers out.

He even brought a few kids back to Glenda for their final judgment.

And with every trip, he felt something shift.

He wasn't the quiet kid in the background anymore.

He had a role.

He had authority.

Within a year, Timmy was learning the projection booth. Thursday nights were the hardest. That's when the reels for the new films arrived and the changeovers had to happen. He learned how to thread the film, check the bulbs, splice the reels so the frames lined up correctly, and change the letters on the marquee. On those nights—especially if none of the current movies were being held over—he had to work really late. Sometimes he was there until one or two in the morning. It was a lot for a young boy who still had to get up early for school the next day.

Eventually, he was trusted with the keys to the theater—left in charge at night. When the last customer left, it was Timmy who turned off the lights, locked the doors, and carried the deposit to the bank drop box. After every showing, he cleaned the theaters himself. Armed with a leaf blower, he'd push the trash to the front, sweep it into piles, and mop up the sticky soda spills that clung to the floor like molasses.

It wasn't glamorous.

But it mattered.

Timmy worked at the Ritz through high school and stayed a little while after graduation. Eventually, a new opportunity came—a desk job at a wholesale grocery company. It wasn't exciting. But it was steady.

Still, something about those nights at the theater stuck with him.

The noise. The smell of popcorn. The rush of a crowd.

The sense of belonging.

For a kid who had always lived on the edges of things, the Ritz had offered a stage—not the kind with a spotlight, but one with purpose. With popcorn and power and just enough responsibility to make a kid feel seen.

It was hard work. The kind no one noticed.

But it taught Timmy something—about showing up, about doing a job well even when no one was watching. About making sure things were ready to open again the next day.

Sometimes, God trains you in the quiet corners—behind a popcorn machine, beside a broom, or under the dim glow of a theater marquee. And you don't realize it until later:

You were learning how to serve.

How to lead.

How to stand tall when the lights go out.

41 STICKS AND STONES

Graduation was just around the corner, and everyone seemed to be getting sentimental. Signing yearbooks. Snapping photos in the hallways. Talking about "the good ol' days"—as if they were already fading into some golden past.

But Timmy didn't feel it—the sadness—the sweet, aching nostalgia that seemed to hang in the air like the last note of a song.

While others clung to the halls like home, he was counting the days until he could walk out for good. He wasn't angry. He wasn't bitter. He was just ready.

It's Just Me Lord, Nobody Special

It wasn't because he hated learning—he didn't. In fact, he liked some classes, especially the creative ones. And it wasn't because he didn't care—he cared more than people knew.

But school had always been the place where the bruises added up.

Not the kind that left marks on your skin.

The kind that settled in your spirit.

The kind you carried in silence.

The kind that stayed hidden for years.

And as the end of senior year drew near, Timmy found himself looking back—not to soak in the memories, not to laugh over old stories or circle faces in a yearbook, but to finally understand the weight he was laying down.

The quiet relief of closing a chapter he never asked to be part of.

The strength it took just to make it through.

Timmy used to believe the sayings that he'd been taught. He'd repeat them like a shield:

"Sticks and stones will break my bones, but words will never hurt me," or *"I'm rubber, you're glue—whatever you say bounces off me and sticks to you."*

They sounded strong. Even brave. The kind of words a kid could cling to when the teasing got too loud or the laughter cut too sharp.

But later in life, Timmy would see them for what they were—well-meaning lies dressed up as armor. Words that promised protection but never delivered. Because sometimes— most times—the words hurt worse.

Timmy had been hit with sticks, with rocks, with belts, fly swatters—even a saltshaker above the eye.

Those things left marks—welts, swelling, the sting of skin snapped raw. Ugly reminders, sure—but ones that eventually faded.

The names they called him?

Those didn't fade.

They stuck to him like burrs on a pant leg—small, sharp, and impossible to shake loose.

"Retarded."

"Weird."

"Stupid."

Those were the nice ones. Most were worse—words that can't be repeated in mixed company.

It's Just Me Lord, Nobody Special

They didn't bounce off.

Not even close.

Timmy wasn't rubber—he was glue.

No—super glue.

The kind that holds tight no matter how hard you try to scrub it off.

He carried those names for years, even after the wounds were long gone.

Because you can apply ice to a welt and watch it shrink. But the kind of damage done by words? That settles deeper.

And it tells you something about yourself that you start to believe—that you're nobody.

Nobody special.

That belief didn't come all at once.

It crept in over time.

In little moments.

Like the day in elementary school when the P.E. teacher pointed to the rope.

Timmy still remembered the shame as the other kids scooted up like it was nothing—gripping the thick cord with their hands and legs, scooting upward like little monkeys.

But not Timmy. His arms trembled. His shoes slipped. The coarse rope scraped against his palms as he struggled to pull himself up. His shirt clung to his back with sweat. He barely made it off the ground before sliding back down in defeat.

They laughed.

Some out loud. Some behind their hands. But he could hear it. He could feel it. It was the first time he thought, maybe something's wrong with me.

And if that hadn't been enough, there was the crab game.

That same year, the class was instructed to scoot around the gym floor like crabs, kicking a giant ball back and forth. The echo of squeaky sneakers and rubber thuds bounced off the cinder block walls. It was supposed to be fun.

But fun turned fast.

Someone missed the ball—and kicked Timmy in the face instead. Right in the eye.

The blow landed with a dull, sickening thud. His vision blurred. His face burned—not just from the impact, but from the heat of every eye in the room turning toward him.

They said it was an accident. Maybe it was. Maybe it wasn't.

It's Just Me Lord, Nobody Special

But Timmy went home that day with a black eye. The swelling came first. Then the purple. No one got in trouble. No one said sorry. And no one checked on the boy in the back row with the bruise—and the questions.

He didn't know it at the time, but that moment was a preview.

A glimpse of what was coming.

Because later, in junior high, the cruelty stopped pretending to be accidental.

It took on a routine.

A rhythm.

It happened every day in music class.

While the teacher was busy with sectionals or working with the altos, Timmy sat to the side, tracing the edge of his music folder with his finger. The room smelled like dust and adolescence. The upright piano creaked when the teacher shifted on the bench.

That's when it would happen.

There was one boy in particular who thought it was funny to spit on him. Not by accident. Not once or twice. Every single day.

He'd purse his lips and shoot a stream of spit between his front teeth like a water gun, aiming for Timmy's shirt or the back of his neck.

Sometimes he'd bring a straw from the lunchroom and use it to fire spit wads when the teacher wasn't looking. They landed with a wet splat. The sound alone made Timmy flinch.

The boy didn't care who saw—as long as he got a laugh. And usually, he did.

Timmy didn't say anything. Not to the teacher. Not to his classmates. What was the point?

He knew nothing would happen. No one would make it stop.

So, he sat there, wiping spit from his neck, pretending not to notice.

Every music class became a countdown. Just make it through today. Just ignore him. Just disappear.

And all the while, the message was loud and clear:

You're a target.

You don't matter.

You're not worth defending.

Later in high school—it was even more violence.

Someone Timmy thought was a friend ran up behind him in the hallway and punched him square in the face before disappearing into the crowd. No warning. No reason. Just a hit and run.

Other boys thought it was funny to flick his ears—sneaking up behind him in class, thumping his earlobes, and ducking away, shouting "Dumbo, Dumbo!" before a teacher could spot them.

He didn't report it. He didn't bother.

He just absorbed it. Silently.

Like someone who stopped expecting better.

Because the damage had already been done.

And not all of it came from classmates.

Some of the worst of it came from home.

From voices that should've known better.

And didn't.

Timmy couldn't always tell where the teasing ended, and the truth began. But deep down, a quiet belief was forming:

He didn't matter.

Not like the others.

Not in the ways that counted.

He smiled when he was hurting. He stayed quiet when he wanted to scream. He tried to be good. He tried to be invisible. But nothing seemed to stop it.

And so, over time, he believed it.

He wasn't the fastest. He wasn't the smartest. He wasn't the favorite.

He was just… Timmy.

Nobody special.

And now, standing on the edge of graduation, he wasn't mourning the end of something beautiful.

He was breathing through the end of something painful.

Because for the first time, it felt like maybe—just maybe—he could write the next part himself.

He used to say, *"Sticks and stones may break my bones…"*

But he knew—It wasn't the sticks that broke him. It wasn't the stones.

It was the silence.

The smirks.

The names.

The feeling of being unwanted.

It's Just Me Lord, Nobody Special

Unimportant.

Unseen.

He bore the bruises—through every year of school.

Just not on his skin.

42 Grandpa Taylor

Grandpa Taylor was the kind of man you didn't forget. Not because he was loud—he wasn't. Not because he was flashy—he wasn't that either. But because he had a presence about him.

He was the kind of man who was going to tell you his opinion, whether you wanted to hear it or not. And once he got to talking, you could count on a few things—he would cough through half the conversation, he'd probably slip in a story—and if you were lucky, he'd leave you laughing so hard your sides hurt.

It's Just Me Lord, Nobody Special

Timmy noticed it when he was little—Grandpa Taylor was missing a finger. One day, curiosity got the better of him, and he finally asked, "Grandpa, what happened to your finger?"

Without skipping a beat, Grandpa held up his hand and said, "I stuck it up my nose, and a booger bit it off!"

Now, a lot of grown-ups would have just told the truth. Not Grandpa. He let Timmy sit there, trying to figure out if that was even possible. And to this day, that explanation is a whole lot more fun than the real one, which Timmy still doesn't know.

Grandpa Taylor had a way of doing things his own way. His overalls were practically a uniform—he wore them everywhere except for church. And even then, you knew it was still him because of that flat-top haircut—neatly trimmed, sharp as a fresh-cut field.

In his earlier years, he was a chain smoker, and as a result, he spent most of his life hacking up his lungs. Timmy could still picture it—Grandpa, sitting back in his brown recliner, coughing so hard it sounded like he was about to keel over… and then, without missing a beat, launching straight into a story.

And what stories they were.

One of his favorites was Old Lady McGuire. He'd rattle it off like a song, never missing a beat:

Old Lady McGuire jumped in the fire,

The fire was so hot she jumped in the pot.

The pot was so little she jumped in the kettle.

The kettle was so black she jumped in the crack.

The crack was so high she jumped in the sky.

The sky was so blue she jumped in the canoe.

The canoe was so long she jumped in the pond.

The pond was so deep she jumped in the creek.

The creek was so shallow she jumped in the tallow.

The tallow was so hard she jumped in the lard.

The lard was so soft she jumped in the loft.

The loft was so rotten she jumped in the cotton.

The cotton was so white she stayed all night.

Timmy never got tired of hearing it.

And then there was Old Sam Sucket.

Grandpa really enjoyed that one. So much, in fact, that he'd recite it at lightning speed, rattling off verse after verse, his voice getting faster and faster until it became a blur of words that no one but him could understand.

Timmy tried. He really did. But no matter how many times he heard it, he could never keep up.

"Old Sam Sucket swapped his wife for a duck egg..." Something about a yoke. Something about a ladder. And then—just like that—Timmy was lost.

Maybe that was the fun of it. Maybe Grandpa never really expected anyone to understand—he just wanted to see how long they could pretend they did before giving up.

And maybe, just maybe, that's where Timmy's love for performing first started.

In the backyard, Grandpa Taylor would always have a vegetable garden, and in it, he planted turnips. Most folks picked them, peeled them, cooked them.

Timmy would pick them, rinse them off with the garden hose, and eat them like an apple.

Grandpa never stopped him. Just let him chomp away, shaking his head.

But not all of Grandpa's ideas worked out so well.

Like the time he took Timmy with him to a friend's house and thought it would be fun to set him on top of a bareback donkey.

Now, Grandpa probably thought it'd be a harmless little ride.

The donkey had other plans. Before Timmy could even settle in,

the donkey bucked, sending him flying.

Grandpa felt awful about it, but Timmy figured it was just one

more story to tell.

And speaking of rides, Grandpa had an old station wagon—

the kind with the hidden seats in the far back. Timmy loved

sitting back there, staring out the back window, watching the

world disappear behind them. It felt like its own little adventure.

Tucked away in a time when seatbelts were optional—when road

trips were the best kind of freedom.

Time has a way of catching up with us all.

Grandpa Taylor spent his final years in a nursing home,

Alzheimer's slowly taking away the sharp mind that had once

spun so much folklore.

It was hard to watch. The man who had once told Old Sam

Sucket faster than anyone could follow… now struggled to

remember the people who loved him most.

But even as his memory faded, something about his

presence never did.

It's Just Me Lord, Nobody Special

Timmy knew he was still in there—the man with the flat-top haircut, the opinions, the laughter, and the stories.

And then came the night before his funeral.
Timmy was sitting on the side of Grandma Taylor's bed, consoling her in her grief, when a group of her church family arrived. They had come to pray with her, to surround her with love in the hardest moment of her life.

And then—after the prayer—they began to sing.
While I was praying, somebody touched me...

The melody rose, gentle at first, filling the room with a warmth that seemed to push back the sorrow.
While I was praying, somebody touched me...

Timmy sat there, his head bowed, his heart heavy. But as the voices continued, something stirred deep within him.
While I was praying, somebody touched me...
Must've been the hand of the Lord.

The presence of God moved in like a whisper at first—then like a flood.
Tears welled in Timmy's eyes. He wasn't just hearing the words. He was feeling them.

And then came the chorus—

Glory, glory, glory, somebody touched me…

A lump formed in his throat.

Glory, glory, glory, somebody touched me…

Timmy's hands gripped the edge of the bed.

Glory, glory, glory, somebody touched me…

Must've been the hand of the Lord.

And that's when it happened.

In that tiny bedroom, with voices raised in worship, with grief thick in the air, Timmy felt it. Something powerful. Something undeniable.

Tears streamed down his face as a warmth flooded his heart, a presence so real he couldn't ignore it.

And in that moment—right there, in the middle of grief and loss—Timmy received the gift of the Holy Ghost.

It was as if, even in passing, Grandpa Taylor was still shaping the journey.

And as Timmy walked away that night, he carried more than just memories.

He carried a calling.

43 Grandma Taylor's Bible

I t was small. Simple. Nothing fancy. But the moment you stepped inside, you felt it—warmth, peace, something steady in a world that wasn't.

At Grandma Taylor's house, you would usually find her relaxing in her recliner, a worn Bible resting in her lap—its pages soft from years of turning. The corners were dog-eared, the cover cracked, the leather faded by time and touch.

It was the same Bible she had read from every morning, the same one she brought to church, the same one she had prayed over for decades. Her thumb had passed over certain verses so many times the ink had faded.

It's Just Me Lord, Nobody Special

Back then, Timmy didn't understand what that Bible meant. He just knew it was important to her. A part of her. Like her glasses, or the soft pink robe she wore on chilly mornings.

But now? He knows.

Because that Bible wasn't just words on a page. It was the prayers she had prayed over her family. It was the whispered petitions she had sent up for a little boy who didn't yet know how much he needed them. It was a living document—creased, marked, and tear-stained—a testimony to battles fought in silence.

And when she wasn't reading, she was humming. A quiet, familiar tune—sometimes an old hymn, sometimes just a melody only she knew. Songs with no lyrics, just feeling. The kind of humming that settled your soul.

But no matter what, it always made Timmy feel safe.

She had a way of making the simplest things special. Like rice pudding. She didn't just cook it—she perfected it. Creamy. Warm. Topped with just the right amount of cinnamon.

And coffee? Well—she had a trick for that too. She'd pour it into a saucer, let it cool just a bit, then sip it from the edge— slow and careful. Deliberate.

Timmy watched her do it so many times, it became second nature to him. Even now, if you ask him, he'll tell you—coffee just tastes better that way.

Everything at Grandma's house had a rhythm. A stillness. She moved slow—not because she was weak, but because she wasn't in a hurry. Timmy often thought the world moved too fast, but not here. Here, you listened for the wind. You watched the clouds. You waited on the Lord.

There was a day Timmy remembered clearer than most—a stormy afternoon spent at her house, the kind where the sky turned dark before supper and the wind swept the dust off the gravel like it had somewhere to be.

The stereo console sat just beneath the big picture window, its lid propped open, spinning a 33 RPM record of Jimmy Swaggart. His voice poured out through the speakers—full of piano and gravel and gospel lyrics. Songs that made you weep without knowing why.

The curtains were pulled wide so Grandma could see everything. She never wanted to miss what might be coming down that road—or out of that sky.

Outside, thunder cracked, and the clouds bruised over. Lightning split the heavens wide—and Timmy flinched.

He didn't like storms much. Never had. But Grandma didn't even blink. She just sat in her chair, calm and steady, hands folded in her lap, eyes fixed on the horizon like she was waiting on someone.

"Grandma," he asked, "why don't storms scare you?"

She smiled, still watching the clouds. "Because," she said, "this could be the cloud that Jesus is coming back on."

And she meant it.

She had spent her whole life watching the clouds.

Then there were the nights spent at her house. When the sun went down and the crickets began their nightly symphony, she and Grandpa Taylor would take him to church.

Not just any church. An old country Pentecostal church— the kind with hardwood floors and an upright piano that never quite stayed in tune. Where the singing wasn't polished, but it was real. Where the pews were hard—but the Spirit was soft. Where people prayed like they expected heaven to listen.

And at that church, Timmy felt something he didn't yet have words for. A pull. A whisper. A presence.

He wouldn't fully understand it for years. But looking back, he can see it now.

God was there. Just like He was in Grandma's house—in her recliner—in the quiet moments when she prayed over that well-worn Bible.

Years later, when Grandma Taylor passed away, that Bible was entrusted to Timmy. He received it just as she had left it— pages fragile, spine held together with black electrical tape.

Worn from time. Worn from love.

And now, when he holds it in his hands, he knows—he wasn't just holding a book. In his hands, he held the legacy she left behind. A roadmap. A compass. A promise.

A reminder that God had been drafting his story long before he ever knew it.

Because Grandma Taylor knew something he didn't.

She knew that the boy sitting at her table, sipping coffee from a saucer… the one flipping through her Bible, too young to grasp its weight… had a calling on his life.

And she prayed him right into it.

It's Just Me Lord, Nobody Special

Grandma Taylor didn't just pray for Timmy. She prayed him forward—into a future he couldn't yet see. She never traveled far herself, but her prayers did.

And years later, those prayers would echo across state lines, through open doors, and into churches, camps, and cities all over North America.

Because somewhere along the way... That barefoot boy with skinned-up knees and a Bible full of promises became a man on a mission—just as she'd always believed he would.

Not because he was special. But because she believed in a God who was.

44 WHERE IN THE WORLD IS TIM RIMMER?

Decades have passed.

It's been a long time since Timmy ran barefoot through the fields of Arkansas, climbed the billboard in Aunt Mary Bell's yard, and raced his bike down roads paved with pea gravel.

So much has changed since then.

For starters, nobody calls him Timmy anymore.

Well, almost nobody.

Only those who grew up close to him still do.

It's Just Me Lord, Nobody Special

Somewhere along the way, the wide-eyed barefoot kid with scraped-up knees and a head full of big dreams grew into Tim—a husband, a father, a grandfather.

They say hindsight is 20/20.
But sometimes, it takes decades—and the quiet prayers of a faithful grandmother—for the picture to come into focus.

Looking back now, Tim doesn't just see a life that unfolded. He sees a life that was guided.

From the outside, it might look like a man who's traveled far and wide, preaching with puppets and props, standing in churches, camps, and conventions across the country.

But those who know the real story—know it started with a prayer.

In 2014, after years of serving, Tim and his wife Yvonne took the biggest leap of their lives.
They walked away from the security of a steady paycheck, a 401(k), and a retirement plan—not because it was easy, but because the call of God was undeniable.
With nothing but a trailer, some puppets, tubs full of object lessons, and a whole lot of faith, they hit the road full-time.
No backup plan. No promises.

Just trust.

And God made a way.

They've stood in the shadow of history—Niagara Falls thundering down in a display of God's power, the Statue of Liberty standing tall as a symbol of freedom, the Alamo where men once stood their ground, the Grand Canyon stretching vast and deep, a testament to creation itself.

And yes—even stopped by the biggest ball of twine in Minnesota, because not every moment in ministry has to be serious to be sacred.

But the real landmarks weren't the ones on the map.

They were the kids kneeling at altars.

The teens who laughed at Sunflower, then cried during the altar call.

The parents who whispered, "Thank you. My child needed this."

Over 10,000 souls—young and old—have come to Jesus through the ministry Tim and Yvonne built on faith.

And if you listen closely, you can almost hear it—the soft rustle of pages turning in Grandma Taylor's Bible.

The whispered prayers of a woman who saw it all coming, even when Tim didn't.

Because she believed before he ever did.

But make no mistake, this journey wasn't easy.

The early years of marriage were a battlefield of expectations.

Family pressure. Religious differences. The constant tug-of-war over how to raise their kids.

They made the decision not to celebrate Halloween—a simple choice grounded in faith, but one that sparked a final blow-up.

That was the breaking point.

It was time to go.

But they were already facing financial hardship because of their youngest son's diagnosis: Hirschsprung's disease.

Surgery. Stress. Sleepless nights.

Medical bills that stacked higher than their faith—some days.

And yet... somehow, God provided.

They didn't go without.

They didn't go hungry.

There was always just enough.

In 2000, they packed up everything they owned, left Arkansas behind, and moved to Tennessee.

Not just to escape pressure—but to walk in obedience.

To build something that was fully theirs.

To raise their family under God's covering, not man's control.

And now, decades later, Tim doesn't look back with regret. He looks back with awe.

Not at what he built—but at what God built through him.

Because obedience may cost you something...

But it always leads to something greater.

And somewhere in Heaven, an old woman with a Bible in her lap is smiling—because everything she saw in prayer, everything she believed in faith, came to pass.

But the greatest blessing?

Not the miles traveled.

Not the history seen.

Not even the countless lives changed.

It's knowing that when you follow God's will—when you trust Him, even when it's hard—He will always take you *farther along* than you ever imagined.

And looking back now, Tim wouldn't change a thing.

From backwoods ditches to Sunday school altars...

It's Just Me Lord, Nobody Special

From crawling out of wreckage to climbing into a calling…

It's been a journey.

And now, Timmy can finally see what he couldn't always see then—that every bump, bruise, blessing, and battle was part of the plan.

Because God doesn't waste anything.

Not even the hard stuff.

Especially not the hard stuff.

45 FINAL REFLECTION

It's funny how, at the time, we don't always recognize the moments that shape us.

We don't always see the purpose in the struggles.

But looking back, it becomes clear.

There was a little boy who got picked last.

A boy who stared at the clouds in the outfield, wondering if he'd ever belong.

A boy who stood in the cold, watching his house burn to the ground.

A boy who was picked up in a trailer by a roaring tornado… and lived to talk about it.

It's Just Me Lord, Nobody Special

A boy who ran his fingers over a tattered Bible, not knowing the prayers inside would carry him through life.

Looking back, it would be easy to say these were just moments.

Just childhood memories.

Just stories from a boy growing up in small-town Arkansas.

But they weren't.

Because that boy?

That boy had no idea each of those moments was shaping something bigger.

That Christmas morning, when Timmy found his microscope sitting unwrapped by the tree, he didn't know.

He didn't know that his curiosity for science would one day become the very thing that captivated thousands of children across the country.

He didn't know that years later, those tiny, bubbling beakers would become object lessons—helping him share the Gospel in ways that kids could see, feel, and understand.

He didn't know that God was planting a seed—one that would grow into a ministry far beyond anything he could have imagined.

Because back then?

Back then, he was just a boy who wanted to see what a booger looked like under a microscope.

And when he walked through the endless rows of vendors at the Canton flea market...

When his eyes landed on that scruffy little monkey puppet... he didn't know.

He didn't know that the moment he picked it up—the moment he handed over his money and named it Josh—his life had just changed.

He didn't know that the hours he spent practicing, making that monkey move, giving it a voice, making it look alive... were preparing him for something greater.

He didn't know that one day ventriloquism would take him across the country—that he would make kids laugh.

That he would use puppets to share the love of Jesus.

He didn't know.

But God did.

And isn't that how it always is?

We don't always see the plan.

We don't always understand why we were picked last, why we

had to start over, why we went through the fire—sometimes literally.

We don't always see the purpose in the moment.

But God does.

He sees the boy hiding under the parachute after being laughed at.

He sees the child sitting in the dark, wondering why love feels so far away.

He sees the young man fighting to believe he's enough.

And He says, "I'm not done with you yet."

We don't always see the purpose in the moment.

But God does.

"For I know the plans I have for you," declares the Lord,

"plans to prosper you and not to harm you,

plans to give you hope and a future."

(Jeremiah 29:11 NIV)

That promise wasn't just for a boy from Arkansas.

It's for you, too.

Because you're not here by accident.

You're not reading this by accident.

No matter where you've been,

No matter what you've faced,

God has been shaping your story all along.

Maybe it was a teacher who said you'd never amount to anything.

Or a parent who never said they were proud.

Maybe it was a moment when you felt small in a room full of people—

Or invisible in a world that never called your name.

But just because no one else saw your worth... doesn't mean God didn't.

He saw every scar, every tear, every whispered prayer.

He saw your courage—

Even when you felt like a coward.

He saw your faith—

Even when all you had left was a whisper of hope.

You see, God specializes in nobodies.

He chooses the weak to shame the strong.

The overlooked to change the world.

He takes the rejected... and redeems them.

He takes the broken... and blesses them.

He takes the ordinary... and makes it extraordinary.

It's Just Me Lord, Nobody Special

And when the time is right,

When the pieces come together,

When you look back and see it clearly...

You'll realize what Timmy did.

Every moment mattered.

Every battle.

Every lesson.

Every scar.

And in the quiet of the night, as you get down on your

knees to pray, maybe—just maybe—you'll say the same words

he did:

"Hello, Lord... it's just me. Nobody special."

But just like Timmy learned—and just like you will too...

God has never seen you that way.

To Him,

You were always

Somebody special.

And now you know...

The rest of the story. Good day!

Afterword

If you made it this far, thank you.

Not just for reading—but for listening.

For sitting through the hard stuff, the funny stuff, and the stuff that didn't always tie up neatly.

I didn't write this book because I had it all figured out.
I wrote it because, for most of my life, I didn't.

I was just a barefoot boy from rural Arkansas.
A quiet middle child with a head full of questions and a heart that often felt too big for the world around him.
I wasn't the strongest. Or the fastest. Or the funniest.
I wasn't anyone people would have expected to grow up and write a book.

But God isn't limited by expectations.
He's not looking for perfection—He's looking for availability.
And as it turns out, that's something even a nobody can offer.

Somewhere between the bullies and the bedtime stories…
Somewhere between the honeysuckle and the heartbreak…
God was there.

When I didn't feel seen—He saw me.
When I didn't feel heard—He listened.
When I felt forgotten—He remembered.

Not everything in this book was easy to share.
Some parts took years to say out loud.
But if even one person reading this finds comfort, finds hope,
finds Jesus a little closer than they thought—then every page
was worth it.

I wrote this story for the kid who feels like he's always
picked last.
For the girl who walks the hallway at school with her head
down, just hoping to survive the day.
For the adult who's still carrying around the label someone else
slapped on them decades ago.
For the one who's heard *"you'll never amount to anything"* one too
many times.

You are not the names they gave you.
You are not the wounds you carry.
You are not the silence you've been forced to sit in.

You are a child of God.

And even if you feel unseen...

Even if you've prayed that same prayer I used to pray night after night— *"It's just me, Lord. Nobody special"*—
I'm here to tell you, He heard it.

He heard you.

He still does.

If my story has taught me anything, it's that God delights in using ordinary people for extraordinary things.

He picks the overlooked, the underestimated, the unseen.

He doesn't just call the qualified—He qualifies the called.

Looking back now, I can see it clearer than ever.

The pain had a purpose.

The trials made room for testimony.

The stories I once kept quiet are the very ones He's now using to help others find their voice.

And maybe—just maybe—that's the whole point.

Not to be known... but to be useful.

Not to be impressive... but to be honest.

Not to become famous... but to be faithful.

If I could sit across from you right now—just you and me—I wouldn't try to preach.

I'd just tell you what I've come to believe deep down in my bones:

God doesn't overlook people. People overlook people.

But God sees. God remembers. God restores.

Your brokenness doesn't disqualify you.

It prepares you.

It humbles you.

It softens the ground for something holy to grow.

You don't need a pulpit to be used by God.

Sometimes, your story *is* the sermon.

And your healing is the altar call someone else has been waiting on.

So if you've ever felt like a nobody, I hope this story reminded you of something true:

Nobody is nobody to God.

If you've been broken, He's the healer.

If you've been lost, He's the map.

If you've been wandering, He's the welcome.

And if you're standing there, wondering if there's still time for your story to mean something…

There is.

Your story matters.

Your voice matters.

Your heart matters.

Because if God can take a shy, overlooked Arkansas boy with nothing but a pocketful of memories… and turn it into a ministry—

then He can do something just as powerful with yours.

So don't count yourself out.

Don't hang your head.

Don't believe the lie that it's too late or you're too far gone.

You are seen.

You are loved.

And you are part of something far greater than you know.

God's not finished with you.

He never was.

There's more ahead—more than you can imagine.

You may not see it yet, but He's already walking the road in front of you, preparing the next chapter.

You're not too broken.

You're not too ordinary.

And you're certainly not invisible.

You may have been told you're nothing special.

You may have even believed it.

But heaven has never whispered those words over your life.

Heaven calls you chosen.

Heaven calls you beloved.

Heaven calls you by name.

So if all you've got left is a whispered prayer and a little bit of hope...

that's enough.

Because God does His best work in the quiet. In the places no one else sees. In the hearts that keep showing up.

It's just me, Lord. Nobody special.

He knows that voice.

He's heard it before.

And He's listening still.

Thanks for spending time with Timmy.

And thank you for letting me share the journey.

—Tim Rimmer

ABOUT THE AUTHOR

Tim Rimmer lives in Murfreesboro, Tennessee, with his wife of over 30 years, Yvonne. Together, they've raised four children and are proud grandparents to a growing number of grandchildren.

Since 2014, Tim and Yvonne have traveled full-time in children's ministry through their nonprofit, God's Handywork, Using puppets, storytelling, and creative object lessons, they share the message of Jesus with children and families across North America.

Their ministry has taken them from small country churches to large city crusades, but their heart remains the same: to reach one more child with the love of God.

When they're not on the road, they enjoy quiet time at home—resting, recharging, and preparing for the next opportunity to serve. Tim still finds joy in the simple things: southern gospel music, coin collecting, and a good story that makes you laugh and cry at the same time.

The stories in this memoir are more than memories—they're reminders of the faithfulness of God through every season. Through this book, Tim invites you to relive the moments that made him who he is today—offering lessons learned from his own journey.

And perhaps, most importantly, he shares a message of hope:

God has a plan for you, too.

connect with me

I'd love to stay in touch. If you'd like to follow along, here's where you can find me:

Website: www.godshandywork.org

Email: imaclown@godshandywork.org

Social Media: @ghwministries

Available on: Facebook, X, Instagram, TikTok, Linktree, and YouTube

I hope to hear from you soon. Until then—keep believing. Keep daring. Keep trusting that your story matters.